Creativity and Conflict in the Plays of Sam Shepard

Creativity and Conflict in the Plays of Sam Shepard

Jyotirmoy Prodhani

AUTHORSPRESS
Publishers of Scholarly Books

Worldwide Circulation through Authorspress Global Network

First Published 2012

by

Authorspress

Editorial

Q-2A Hauz Khas Enclave,
New Delhi-110 016
e-mail: authorspress@rediffmail.com

Marketing

E-35/103, Jawahar Park
Laxmi Nagar, Delhi-110 092
e-mail: authorspress@rediffmail.com

Creativity and Conflict in the Plays of Sam Shepard

ISBN 978-81-7273-611-8

Printed in India at Srikrishna Offset Printers, Delhi.

To

My father, the late

Sibesh Chandra Prodhani

who valued art and education

and

Prof. Jasbir Jain

who made me ambitious

Preface

Theatre as a genre has traversed a long way. In the last century its form became formidably radical as it entered into the domain of the avant-garde. But then, the jealously cultivated modernist art forms evolved into alienating manifestations. There was an uneasy relationship between the common and the connoisseurs, between the elites and the masses. Paradoxically, both the avant-garde as well as the mainstream lost immediacy with the masses; the first owing to its ultra elitist obsession and the second owing to its conscious deviation towards a stylized reality. Hence, theatre too, like all other art forms, had to find itself an alternative space. In its attempt to reinvent itself, new theatre found itself at a double distance-it was away from the avant-garde as well as the mainstream. It shifted its base beyond the radical as well as the oppressively opulent corridors of the mainstream theatre. It emerged as Off Off Broadway. Robert Schroeder called such theatre as the 'New Theatre from the Underground'.

In one of its reviews, *Time Magazine* wrote, "If plays were put in time capsules, future generations would get a sharp-toothed profile of life in the U.S. in the past decade and a half from the works of Sam Shepard." In fact, with Sam Shepard theatre assumed a new historico-cultural dimension not only pertaining to America alone but also in relations to the changing cultural landscapes of the entire postmodern world. The question of creativity has become an abidingly critical issue as the location and the sustenance of an artist and his art are no longer solely predicated upon the sublime refinement of the artist alone. It has essentially become dependent on the operations of the extraneous forces that regulate and determine the course of artistic creations and their fate in a cultural condition where market predominates. This is where Shepard becomes a quintessential prophet of our time who would take up this particular aspect of creative crisis with which we are so disturbingly familiar as part of our own knowledge of the cultural politics in our respective milieu.

This book would never have evolved had I not been introduced to Sam Shepard by Prof. Jasbir Jain of University of Rajasthan, Jaipur. She was the one who was so extraordinarily kind to me to give some of the most valuable and extremely rare documents on Sam Shepard. She was also the one who had opened a new world for me. In fact, she inspired me to look at Shepard and the question of the crisis of creativity as envisaged by Shepard. I am extremely grateful to her. I am also immensely indebted to the late Prof. E.N. Lall of the North-Eastern Hill University (NEHU), Shilong, who had guided me throughout the course of this work and taught me the value of uncompromising rigour in academic exercises. I also fondly recall Prof. Bella Lall for her affectionate gestures. Prof. Pradip Acharya of Cotton College, Guwahati, has been a constant inspiration for me not only for my academic works but also for understanding of and dealing with life with mature perspective.

I am especially thankful to the American Studies Research Centre (ASRC), Hyderabad, for the Teachers' Study Grant that was extremely crucial in consulting the huge pool of resources in the library and interacting with the scholars and experts to further sharpen the arguments in the book.

While working on this manuscript I was so fortunate to get immense support from Dr. Santosh Kr. Sarkar and Dr. Bharat Bhusan Mohanty of Chilarai College, Golakganj, Assam. My friend Dr. Rajesh Dev is currently in Delhi University extended his cooperation when it was most needed. Dr. Prasenjit Biswas and Dr. Sukalpa Bhattacharjee of NEHU, Shillong, have been very kind to me whenever I was in Shillong in connection with this work. I must acknowledge the preiceless support of my friends, Partha Sarathi Mahanta and Indrani Baura of Guwahati. I am also indebted to my friends at Golakgari Gautam Raoy choudhury, Bapi Sengu Gupta, Depa, Deepak, Jugal and Prarshanta for their tremendous support during the course of my work.

I must express my gratitude to my colleagues in the Dept. of English at NEHU, Tura Campus, for their constant support. Angela Ingty, Jova Marak, Ramona Sangma and especially to my senior colleagues, R.S. Thakur and Prof. Sujata Gurudev for being so motivating and concerned about the development of my work.

My friend Chandra Mouli, a writer and a poet from Hyderabad, showed his enthusiasm for this work and introduced me to Sudarshan Kcherry of Authorspress who was so courteous and generous to immediately go ahead with the publication of this book. I am truly grateful to him.

My wife Preeti Nisha would always instill the much needed confidence in me to believe in my own abilities. My son, little Uddiyan, would in his own way, give life that precious moments of reassurance when I would need them the most against the uncanny rhythms of high and low I encountered during the course of my work. It would not have been possible without my mother's blessings and my younger brother, Nilimoy's, good wishes.

And the last but not the least, my *Almighty*, who had been there beside me all through to empower me with her divine grace and the special blessings of Amma Bhagwan that enabled me to complete this work.

Jyotirmoy Prodhani

Abbreviations

AC	Angel City
CM	Cowboy Mouth
GHD	Geography of a Horse Dreamer
MDB	Mad Dog Blues
MP	Melodrama Play
RTL	Rolling Thunder Logbook
SB-f	Suicide in B-flat
TOC	Tooth of Crime
TW	True West

Contents

1

Introduction

Theatre as Discourse: Postmodern Cultural Politics and Shepard's Plays

I

"In other countries, art has a role and the artist a social position. Not in the U.S. Here art is understood, if at all, only as a commodity ... and artists don't exist until they become something else: celebrities", writes Michael Feingold with an uneasy concern (xix, 1993). In the prevailing condition it is difficult for art to have a sovereign existence of its own for, under the current circumstance it is inherently susceptible to become a commodity, and as a commodity it enters the market to transform into what Baudrillard would call 'simulacra'. In this new context, creativity, the fundamental basis of art, is reformulated following its shift from its traditional praxis. Art becomes a victim of a particular mode of production in a context of a new reality.

There is a peculiar distance between audience and art, vis-à-vis the artist. It is the 'sleep walkers' (Feingold) who keep the system running and who are only attached to the hypnotic media net of TV and movies. While talking about the role of TV in evolving the socio-cultural behaviour in postmodern America, Feingold says, "Falling asleep with the TV on is one of the central images of our culture" (xvi). The obvious passivity of the audience is no longer significant for art because the audience involvement has become an insignificant criterion for such art to sustain and get recognised. It is the corporate sponsors and their endorsement that determine the status and value of art.

In the system, largely occupied by 'sleep walkers', some 'residual perceptions' (Feingold) still remain along its margin where the residents are wide awake, and seriously respond to the issues that annoy them. They are adequately distanced from their milieu and that had enabled them to form a perspective to notice the things which are, for others, too obvious to be noticed. They notice drugs, crime, aggressive market and corporate manipulations. In the cities as well as in the suburbs they notice homeless people, the renegades and, *inter alia*, the hypnotism of the media. They form a community to go together to theatres to produce a collective noise to wake up the others. This is what Sam Shepard would call a 'controlled anarchy.' (qtd. in Carol Rosen '93)

This provocation of noise does not occur in every theatre as it didn't in the Broadway. Provocation of noise requires free expression which was almost impossible in the Broadway, for there, as Feingold would point out, "art (was) embattled on the economic front as well as political", that led to the curtailment of the ambition of taking risks. Therefore, a serious play could not survive in the Broadway, "where nobody (wanted) to be serious." (Feingold xix)

This limitation evokes a counter movement for alternative theatre, which does not require huge resources. Their strength lies in their invincible passion and anger. This dramatic movement the critics have defined as Off Off Broadway – the new theatre, away from the precincts of the mainstream Broadway both in terms of physical and temperamental distance – that turned out to be a source of hope for an embittered nation. Feingold therefore warns, "if the theatre does not grow up, the American public does not grow up either" (xiii). American theatre, according to Feingold, so far failed to attain maturity as an institution by evolving a native theatre tradition of its own. And the kind of theatre that was in force only reflected the nation's general 'commitment to staying immature' – eager consumers of goods by being overgrown babies.

The new theatre captures this time of loss and despair, of confusion, of starvation, of homelessness, of oppression and violence. The collective reaction of this theatre to this reality makes it an angry time. Sometimes explicitly, as in Antonin Artaud and David Mamet; sometimes subtly as in Lanford Wilson, David Rabe and Sam Shepard.

II

Drama is "inherently ideological" writes C.W.E. Bigsby, yet there is a critical reticence about drama in general and American drama in particular. Literary critics, cultural historians, social theorists, who are engaged in studying the evolution of genres in discourse and ideology, find so little to say about theatre. Theatre's achievement has hardly been comprehensively analysed and the genre itself has been accorded rather a marginal position. Drama by virtue of its generic character incorporates a critical reading in the very process of its transmission, and poses a challenge to the establishments through its direct communication with its implied audience.

Language is power, said Foucault, and according to Bigsby, shaping of that language into art is power and the codification of that art in the form of literary history is the source of power (1, 1992). This is one of the central issues that Shepard addresses in his plays. In his plays, which are a kind of metadrama, Shepard tries to critically look at the position of art and artist against a cultural context of ontological complexity. The plays taken up for the present study deal with the position of the artist and his creative endeavours under a condition of forced social silence. The artistic articulations are mutilated or subjected to forceful withdrawals, yet the artist remains a 'central presence', for at least the space is physically occupied by their bodies. At times even the body is withdrawn, as in *Suicide in B-Flat* (1976), making empty spaces more vocal, more powerful a political statement.

One of the major Sam Shepard critics, Ross Wetzsteon, in his essay, "The Genius of Sam Shepard", divided the plays of Shepard in three major categories. First are the early one-acts beginning from 1963/64 to the mid-seventies which include *Rock Garden* (1964), *Icarus's* Mother (1965); *Red Cross* (1966),

La Turista (1960); *Oh!, Calcutta* (1967) and *Tongues* (1978). The plays reflect, what Wetzteon pointed out, "a sense of paranoid despair" (23). Textually the plays are in the form of abstract collages, with lyrical monologues and with stunning visual and verbal imageries.

The second group of plays, as devised by Wetzteon, deals with the visionaries who pursue their emotional identity and spiritual freedom "even if it results in isolation and betrayal" (23). This group of plays includes the plays like *Melodrama Play* (1967); *Mad Dog Blues* (1971); *Cowboy Mouth* (1971); *Bad Dog Beast Bait* (1971); *Tooth of Crime* (1972); *Geography of a Horse Dreamer* (1974); *Angel City* (1976); *Suicide in B-flat* (1976); *Seduced* (1977) and *True West* (1980). In this set of plays Shepard deals with the theme where the artist becomes a cult figure in popular imagination and eventually becomes a victim of his own apotheosis.

In the third category he has included the two great 'family plays', *Curse of Starving Class* (1977) and *Buried Child* (1978) including *True West* (1980). Shepard won his fourth of the tenth Obie awards in 1977 for *Curse* which was followed by the Pulitzer Prize in 1979 for *Buried Child*. The plays focus on the theme of the re-building of private history by redeeming the lost comfort of family – a social institution which was on the verge of total collapse.

In this book I shall attempt to focus on the second category of his plays, which are considered to be the most elusive of Shepard's plays, with the objective of devising a perspective to understand the statements formulated through their dramatic discourses. The focus will be on the crisis of creativity and the conflict in the process of creative encounters in a backdrop of postmodern cultural exigencies; on the question of the subjective location of the artist against the given cultural map and on the issues involved with the discourse of Shepardian aesthetics and concerns as evolved through the distinctive narrative of his plays.

The plays have reflected Shepard's perpetual awareness of his Americanness. The protagonists here are paralogical[1] entities who confront crisis against the silencing mechanism of the new cultural regime. The plays draw attention to the struggle of the protagonists for the retrieval of a space of creative isolation and to escape from a condition of 'unfreedom' (Adorno) onto a liberated space of private landscape.

Shepard expresses a deep commitment to the notion of artist's inexorable attachment to his time and space as well as to the people an artist supposedly addresses. He suggests:

There's more to it than just getting off as an artist, because you know, anybody can make a piece of art admired by any number of people. But what happened between those other people and the artist? Is there really a sense of responsibility in the relationship between the thing you make and the people who come in touch with it ? (qtd. in Ver Meulen 85)

The supposed relationship between the artist and his art and his audience is the central issue that Shepard takes up in the plays belonging to the second group of his plays.

About the creative process, Shepard discusses his personal experience as a playwright in one of his essays. He discusses his method of making deposits and withdrawal from an unconscious "Inner Library" (214) of experience (one of his key concepts regarding the source and process of creativity). He speaks about his characters who appear out of nowhere in three dimensions and begin to speak. He points out that the genesis of his plays lies not in mere ideas but in images. The sense of being from nowhere is a constant preoccupation for the artist protagonists in Shepard. Shepard elaborates the role of images in his own creative process:

The picture is moving in the mind and being allowed to move more and more freely as you follow it. The following of it is the writing part. In other words, I'm taking notes in as much details as possible on an event that's happening somewhere inside me. The extent to which I can follow the pictures and not intervene with my own two cent' worth is where inspiration and craftsmanship hold their real meaning. If I find myself pushing the character in certain direction, it almost always a sure sign that I've fallen back on technique and lost the real thread of the thing. ("Inner Library" 215)

Shepard's protagonists in the plays – the Rock plays (the term used to refer to the plays where the protagonists is a Rock 'n' Roll artist but in the present study the term would be used to refer to the plays where the protagonist is an artist or related to the system of producing art)—reflect one of the perennial Shepardian concerns: 'homelessness'. Shepard says:

> I feel like I've never had a home, you know? I feel related to the country, to this country, and yet at the same time I don't know exactly where I fit in. And the same thing applies to the theatre. I don't know exactly how well I fit into the scheme of things. May be that's good, you know, that I'm not in a niche. But there's always this kind of nostalgia for a place, a place where you can reckon with yourself. ("Inner Library" 215)

This strong sense of alienation, the feeling of being a pariah, despite having a sense of belonging to a country; and the nostalgia for lost memories and history are the distinctive characteristics of Shepard's artist-protagonists.

The artists in Shepard belong to a postmodern domain and they are quintessentially American. They are the products of the special American cultural map. They symbolise a definite cultural role and meaning in their respective images. They are both products and producers of postmodern art. Wetzsteon calls these characters as "shamans" (25). Cowboys, Rock 'n' Roll stars, criminals, jazz musicians, screenplay writers or the mystic figures like Paul Bunyan or Mae West are the characters in Shepard who embark on a search for emotional freedom. "Sometimes", Ross Wetzsteon, writes, "they reach a momentary ecstasy of self fulfillment, but more often than not they are forced to surrender their private vision to the service of public commerce. They are spiritually kidnapped" (25). The vision of the artist and the power of their creative assertions are separated from each other and are distributed between two individuals—the artist and the mafia. The artist has only the dream, the power lies elsewhere. "You got the genius, somebody else got the power" (291), the gambler tells Cody, the dreamer, in *Geography of a Horse Dreamer*.

Shepard himself has been exposed to diverse creative exercises. He has been a drum player in the band, the *Holy*

Modal Rounder, a screenplay writer (*Zabriskie Point* in 1968, *Paris, Texas* in 1984), appears as an actor in the movies like *Days of Heaven* (1981), where he met Jessica Lange and married her later, besides being a poet and a playwright. Shepard, therefore, is well exposed to the process as well as the crises of creativity and the conflict an artist encounters as a creator.

Artist's creative exclusivity is replaced by its reproducibility. Shepard witnesses the time when avant-garde art of high modernism is a defeated event. Modernism, as an intellectual movement, fed by disgust and impatience with the slow and sluggish spaces of change, was a protest against broken promises and dashed hopes with a commitment to radicalism. There was a strong disapproval of the extant state of art and the role assigned to arts in connection to society. It also derided the past and ridiculed its canons and values. Stefan Marowsky, the polish philosohoper of art, mentioned the traits of the avant-garde art of modernism as having a historic sense of accomplishment, the urge to follow the patterns of revolutionary movements, orientation towards collectivism, adoption of common programmes and manifestoes, thus taking self initiatives to become a collective harbinger of time that was yet to come and to work towards the formation of a preliminary blueprint for the future's universal pattern. They took it as their moral duty to show the light to the uninitiated, and paradoxically the avant-garde school could validly claim its exclusivity so long as the teacher and taught are not merged and the difference between the two is not obliterated. Avant-garde always sought the other 'sunk-in darkness' in both intellectual and material sense. But as analysed by Zygmunt Bauman in his book *Post-modernity and Its Discontents* (1997), the modernist movement in general was horrified and appalled when the distinction between avant-garde and the rest was erased, when everything supposedly radical was readily approved and the incomprehensibility of art was neutralised. Anything they produced failed to shock. Thus art and artist suffered from a sense of being insufficiently radical. Avant-garde, then, sought more difficult forms to ensure the most advanced detachment between intellectuals and the laity in order to exclude the masses from the processes of cultural creations. Modernism sought the continuity of the socio-cultural dialectics to be operational within the dichotomy of two classes – "those who can understand and those who cannot" (Bauman, 98). There was concerted move to sustain the difference and as John Carey suggests, the difference was necessary for the assertion of superiority of the learned and the creative: the significance of minority, the intellectuals, was directly proportionate to its ability to outrage and puzzle the masses (*Intellectuals and Masses*).

With the emergence of the arriviste middle class, market soon intervened to subvert the process of modernist creations. The more recondite the art the more potential it became a commodity for the 'art market', because avant-garde art became a symbol of intellectual prestige for the *nouveau riche*, as art came to signify a social distinction. In order to escape from the trap of popular consent and acceptance, as suggested by Umberto Eco, avant-garde champions sought new ventures in extreme forms to transgress its own limits. "The limit of arts lived as a permanent revolution", points out Bauman, "was self-destruction" (100). The ritual of self-destruction was evident when art reached the empty and charred canvases like the erased Rosenberg's drawings; the empty New York Gallery at Yves Klein's private viewing; the hole dugged up by Walter-de-Maria in Kassel; John Cage's silent music; Robert Barry's 'telepathetic exhibition' of empty pages of unwritten poems *et al*. The perdition of avant-garde was affected from both inside and outside. Even the sites for such radical ventures became unavailable forcing modernism to phase out. Hence, Bauman makes the comment, "avant-garde art proved to be modern in intention, yet postmodern in their consequence" (100). Art failed to retain its exclusive autonomy. This is the juncture from where Shepard's plays take off. He contextualises the artists against this background when new identities and patterns are emerging for art and new ideas are being invented for all new aesthetic discourses.

New artistic inventions are not meant to chase out and replace the extant ones, but to join the others, finding some elbow room in the notoriously over crowded artistic stage. The entire structural pattern is altered where synchronicity of art has been replaced by a diachronic "co-presence (which) takes the place of succession and the perpetual present replaces history – competition takes over from the crusade" (Bauman 100). Artists do not have to pretend to have undertaken a mission of political advocacy or of cultural prophesying of pseudo truths (in *Cowboy Mouth* Slim is forced by Cavale to become a prophet but Slim ostensibly failed to comply with the proposal).

One of the fundamental conditions under which postmodern art has to survive is competition which leads to the subsequent impossibility of collective actions, coordination of ideas and structures, and evolving of a disciplined pattern that eventually rules out collective negotiation of rules and canons. Art, as well as the process of creation, becomes anarchic. Hoss laments in *Tooth of Crime* (1972) that there is no 'teacher', hence, it is 'without a code' and it becomes 'just a crime', because, there is "No art involved. No technique. No sense of mastery" (*TOC*, 29). Hoss becomes a classic example of the one who justifies the declared fate of the postmodern artist – "maximal impact and instant obsolescence" (George Steiner).

The stratifying power of art now no longer belongs to the artist, nor to the artistic creations. It is the 'site' at which art is viewed or purchased is what that counts, and the price it commands is what that determines the qualitative value of art. Thus a work of art does not differ from other marketable commodities. Saul Kimmer, the Hollywood producer in *True West* determines the fate of art by taking part in the executions of their purchases. Austin, the established screenplay writer immediately becomes an irrelevant writer as soon as Kimmer decides to drop his script, and Lee, whose story is bought by Kimmer impulsively for an absurdly huge amount, becomes a recognised artist instead. But Austin warns Lee and exhorts him to bring down his excitement after having sold his story: "You don't come up with a winner on your first time, they cut your head off. They don't give you a second chance" *The West*, 40). The inevitable involvement of the artist in a fatal competition is a stark reality of the postmodern cultural map. (The urge to create a work of art is essentially one of the most important ambitions. "The ambition behind this ambition", says Miss Scoons, "is no different from any other ambition. To kill. To win. To get on top". (*Angel City,* 31)

III

The present day art is distinctively separated from the actual social reality. These arts, suggests Bauman, have elevated themselves into a *sui generic* reality. Thus art too shares the plight of postmodern culture in its entirety (101). Jean Baudrillard has described this as the culture of *simulacrum* and not representation. Art itself becomes one of the many realities and each of them has definite mechanisms of proclaiming authenticity and the comparative qualities of those realities are extremely difficult to determine. It becomes almost impossible to find out relative authenticity of the art pieces, the 'more real', from the many realities that are simultaneously available. The difference between the primary and the secondary blurs irrevocably, even the origin and the copy become redundant like the paintings of Andy Warhol. This situation Baudrillard explains in terms of a 'psychosomatic disease', where the patient's pains are quite real but the reality of illness may be a questionable truth. The situation operates through the dynamics, as Baudrillard states, of "code and reproduction" – reproduction which is itself an "original" (in Lechte 235). When Hoss, the defeated rock star in *Tooth of Crime* (1972), screams, "I got my own ... Original. I'm my own man. Original" (*ToC,* 620), Crow, the master adapter, perfectly gets into Hoss's walking style and his disposition forcing Hoss to struggle to change his own style in order to remain original, but he eventually fails to do so. The 'original' (Hoss) and the reproduction (Crow) become redundant. The 'originality' of Hoss could have ensured him a victory in the combat but the referee credits winning points to Crow because 'originality' evades Hoss as it can be perfectly reproduced—"How can you give points to liar", the referee explains coolly, "I don't. I give to the winner." (*TOC* 58)

Baudrillard provides a perspective by pointing out that natural object is no longer credible; the codes have raised simulation to an unprecedented importance in social life. This provides false assumptions and power to the individual involved in the process of simulation, because the code that is associated with the process bypasses reality creating a new situation, which Baudrillard calls 'reversibility'. It entails disappearance of all finalities as it does in case of 'simulation' and 'simulacra'.

Media is a crucial aspect in the process of simulation. About the false power that the process provides, Shepard says, "Dealing with the media makes you believe that you have an importance beyond your actual importance. It leads to a lot of false assumptions about who are you" (qtd. in Ver Meulen 86). One becomes a victim of media simulated pretension.

Origin of things becomes a set of coded signals and gets reduced into a framework of numbers and formulations, hence, reversibility becomes an intrinsic possibility. The last original produced can be perfectly reproduced. Crow in *TOC* masters these codes and shows Hoss the process that operates to blur the difference between himself, Rod Stewart and Bob Dylan:

> move yer head like Rod Stewart ... Listen to Hendricks ... sound like a Dylan, sound like a Jagger ... wear in' a shag now, looks like a fag now. (Crow in *TOC*, 62/3)

In this system of simulation and reproduction the difference between the real and the reproduced is erased. In its extreme form even death becomes a reversible event, which implies that death does not really happen as in *Suicide in B-Flat* (1976) where the death of Niles failed to enable him to escape his own 'simulacra', or in the case of Henry Heckamore in *Seduced* (1977), where, despite his desperate bid to die, he keeps on being reproduced.

Shepard takes up one of the most crucial aspects of postmodern creativity and locates the artists in a zone of anarchic crisis and conflict. As Baudrillard points out, the era of the code is all pervasive and penetrates each aspect of life wherein the opposites begin to collapse and 'everything becomes undecidable' and is caught in an aporia. The beautiful and the ugly in fashion, the left and the right in politics, the true and the false in media, authenticity and falsity in art, the pure and the spurious in creativity – all become interchangeable in the era of reproduction and simulation. The artists in Shepard still continue to search for the elusive state of creative sanity through the states of implosive violence. The characters are transmigrated into the realm of hyper reality. In this state of hyper-reality the difference between the image and the actual is permanently effaced. Rabbit Brown discloses in *Angel City*, "You're on the silver screen, buddy. You've been captured in celluloid and you'll never get out" (*AC*, 52) and this involves, in Rabbit Brown's own admission, annihilation of the reality ("You can't mix real life with the movies" (*AC*, 46).

Shepard locates the struggle of artists around a 'territory of language'. The struggle for the control of the linguistic territory is most successfully featured in *Tooth of Crime* where Hoss and Crow are engaged in a fatal fight in order to establish the superiority of their respective languages. Their private vernacular becomes the basic foundation to claim superiority over others. They readily admit their limitations within their respective languages. It is the voice, the sound and language that form the 'turf' of 'power' without which Hoss admits to have nothing ("something subtle like the sound of his voice could thro me off', Hoss in *TOC*, 37). Thus the subject in Shepard, like any other subject for that matter, is part of a linguistic system which is; by virtue of its own characteristic; decentered, arbitrary, and incomplete hence, by applying the Lyotardian paradigm, it can be said that subject too is fragmented, decentered, protean and incomplete. In fact, Shepard himself has given a candid description of his characters – "character" instead of a "whole character" is a "fractured whole with bits and pieces. In other words, more in terms of collage construction or jazz improvisation." (in his "Notes to the Actors" in *Angel City* 6)

Lyotard can help provide a perspective to look at Shepard's plays especially through his notion of "paganism" and "Paralogy". He writes in *Postmodern Condition*, "Let us wage war on totality, let us be witnesses to the unpreventable; let us activate the differences ..." (82). He points out that the principles of paganism are heteronomy and multiplicity which address the issue as to how fragmented, decentred and changing can a subject be and yet can retain the basic elements of his self. In Shepard's dramatic world the unifying thread to hold together diverse subjects in the formation of a community is pronouncedly ineffective, for the individuals are pitted against each other with their respective contesting interest. Hence, all attempts of forming a coalition would either temporarily succeed or, for sure, would fail absolutely. In *Tooth*, the formation of any consensus has been an abortive attempt right from the beginning. Consensus leads to a compromise, which can assure survival not sovereignty. The failure of such unifying attempts continue to be the dominating theme in Shepard's plays. The characters constantly refuse to settle the boundaries of signification and thereby the protagonists wage the battles against this encroachment of terror. Lyotard attacks terror both in terms of its politics and aesthetics. Politically, the subject resists continuation of injustice; aesthetically he resists the attempts of stifling the alternative expressions.

The artists' language inherently resists obligation to structuring forces, hence, their language is indeterminate – like that of the dream of Cody in *Geography* which is purely arbitrary and beyond all predications and controls. Thus creative discourses essentially stand as counterbalance against all meta-discourses of the terrorising forces – the normalising apparatuses of state-sponsored cultural institutions.

The artists seem to have taken up the mission of setting up of an 'open system' in Lyotardian sense. This is translated as 'turf' by Hoss (*Tooth*); 'environment' by Cody (*Geography*); 'life' by Henry (*Seduced*); and 'anonymity' by Niles (*Suicide*). The system they aspire to reach out is a place where they can be heard in which we can include, as Lyotard says, the 'deferent', the unpreventable, which can accommodate expressions alien to the dominant *phrase regimen*—an 'open system'. The artists, however, in Shepard, seldom succeed in achieving this state of 'open system'. He is inexorably engaged in a struggle against the terrorism of the dominant system that prevents him from achieving any centrality within the institutional territory of cultural and political discourses.

'Terror", as defined by Lyotard, "is the efficiency gained by eliminating, or threatening to eliminate a player from language game one shares with him" (63). The open system, on the other hand, provides space where there is no metalinguistic dominance. The approach to approximate this state of open system requires pagan retrogression on the part of the subjects to 'legitimise' the unpreventable and the 'uncivilised'. The artists in Shepard wage this anti-authoritarian war to establish the legitimacy of the 'pariah', the 'outsider', and ensure the political validity of their voice against the canonical discourses of social and cultural order.

The protagonists take the path of paralogy (dissension), which is a part of their pagan selves that strive to fight against all impositions and evolve the ideas for alternative expressions. Within the territory of 'terror' they can only *create* through paralogy and paganity. Lyotard argues, 'invention is always born of dissension'. Creativity being an exercise of invention is predicated upon this fundamental condition of dissension – legitimation of instabilities. The artists, therefore, take a stance to oppose the metanarrtive simulated through sophisticated technical means and mechanisms. As Lyotard describes, postmodern knowledge is a search for instabilities, so is the search of the postmodern artist, who looks for the means to destabilise the ordered structure. This is the means of disempowering the authorities and legitimising as well as reinforcing the incommensurable. For Lyotard, "postmodern knowledge is then not simply a tool of the authorities; it refines our sensitivity to differences and reinforces our ability to tolerate the incommensurable. *Its principle is not expert's homology, but the inventor's paralogy*" (Lyotard xxv, italics mine).

Paralogy aesthetically promotes artistic inventiveness of free spirits and it makes individuals sensitive to, and tolerant of differences. Thus artist's dissensus or paralogy, in the Lyotardian sense, is a continuous search for new moves and expressions to challenge the consensus of dominant paradigm.

Cody's conceptual poetry in the form of his dream in *Geography* is a search for predicting the 'winners' to subvert a particular institutionalised system, which turns catastrophic for the people who are involved in that system. They, therefore, try to force Cody to reduce his visionary poems as a means for their personal gain. As the visions fail to remain a challenge to the system, Cody as an artist loses the power to invent any more.

This book looks for the subjective position of the artists in a geography of contesting forces. It tries to locate the spaces where the artist fragments into multiple entities, their expressions break down as unintelligible utterances and gestures become asemantic as their identities fall apart. In Shepard artists' apparent defeat is the source of his creative redemption, and his destruction is the process through which he regenerates his artistic self. Here I shall make attempts to examine the process of creativity in the post avant-garde and postmodern cultural condition which is not a mere expression of a self but a political articulation through which idioms are invented to challenge the canonical paradigms. They not only warrant an analysis but also an intimate understanding for the, to borrow a Rortian term, 'redecoration of artist as a community'. In Shepard's plays, they resign themselves to defeat only to justify their 'small narrative' (*petit recit*, as Lyotard would call it) as a legitimate reality of a new cultural map which redescribes the socio-cultural territory of a given nation. They are a predominant presence in this cultural universe, for they are not mere artists, they are Shamans engaged in the exotic ritual of exorcising the dubious elements from the sites of art – West, Hollywood, myths, history, music, writing and dreams.

This study has taken up those plays where artists are the providers of these sites of art. Kosmo, Yahoodi in *Mad Dog Blues*, Lee in *True West* are involved in the exercise of redefining the West. Hoss in *Tooth*, Niles in *Suicide*, Slim in *Cowboy Mouth*, Duke in *Melodrama Play* are the musicians who betray the ultimate act of aesthetic challenge and face the emphatic counter challenge from the establishment. Cody in *Geography* is a dreamer, the inventor of conceptual poetry, who encounters the oppressive subjugation by the corporate world. Rabbit Brown, Scoons in *Angel City*, Henry Heckamore in *Seduced* Lee and Austin in *True West* are involved with the biggest "art making industry" – Hollywood—wherein, like Shepard himself, they are reduced into minions. They realise that the existence of an artist within such a mega system is only a survival through compromises not only with their artistic principles but also with the reality of their own physical selves.

Despite such repressive politics the artists are victorious as creative individuals. They triumphantly resist all interpellations and register the legitimacy of their dissension by keeping behind a trail of hope for the physically less powerful, and formidably establish the supremacy of 'inventor's paralogy' as the most powerful means for authentic survival. They may be "defeated" but they are not "destroyed".

Note and Reference

1. Frederick Jameson in his Foreword to Lyotard's *Postmodern Condition: A Report on Knowledge* (1984), interprets Lyotardian 'paralogy' precisely as a search not for consensus but for 'instabilities'. He explains paralogism as a practice in which the point is not to reach at an agreement but to undermine from within the very framework in which previous knowledge had been conducted. (vii-xxi). Lyotard himself, on the basis of own formulations, rejects Habermasian principle of consensus as an inadequate criterion off validation. Firstly, consensus presupposes an agreement between men described as 'knowing intellects' and free wills and this agreement is obtained through dialogue, but this Habermasian formulation is, according to Lyotard, is based on the validity of the narrative of emancipation. Secondly, consensus is a component of a system that manipulates component in order to legitimise the system itself, i.e. the existing power structure (see Lyotard, 1984 pp 60-61).

Works Cited

Bauman, Zygmunt. *Postmodernity and Its Discontent.* New York: New York UP, 1997.

Bigsby, C.W.E. *Modern American Drama: 1945-1990.* Cambridge: Cambridge UP, 1992.

Chubb, Kenneth. "Metaphors, Mad Dogs and Old Time Cow Boys: An Interview with Sam Shepard". Ed. Bonnie Maranca, *American Dream: The Imagination of Sam Shepard.* New York: Performing Arts Journal Publications, 1981.

Feigngold, Michael. *Grove New American Theatre.* New York: Grove Press, 1993.

Freedman, Morris. *American Drama in School Context.* Carbondale, Southern Illinois UP, 1971.

Lyotard, Jean Francois. *Postmodern Condition: A Report on Knowledge.* Tr. Geoff Benington and Brian Masumi. Manchester: Manchester UP, 1984.

Rogoff, Gordon. "America Screened". *Village Voice.* 17 December, 1985.

Shepard, Sam. "Language, Visualisation and the Inner Library". Ed. Bonnie Maranca, *American Dream: The Imagination of Sam Shepard..* New York: Performing Arts Journal Publications, 1981.

_____. *Tooth of Crime.* In *Sam Shepard: Seven Plays.* New York: Bantam Books, 1981.

_____. *Angel City and Other Plays.* New York: Urizen Books, 1977.

_____. *Geography of a Horse Dreamer, Suicide in B-flat, Seduced, Fool for Love and other Plays.* New York: Bantam Books, 1984.

_____. *The Mirror of Production.* Trans. Mark Poster. St. Louis: Telos Press, 1975.

Wetzsteon, Ross. "The Grimus of Sam Shepard." *New York*, 24 November, 1980

2

Drama of the Margin: Off Off Broadway and Sam Shepard

With the arrival of the Off Off Broadway theatre, America's search for a dramatic form of its own seemed to have been achieved. Ironically, America could not find its own dramatic form in the opulent corridors of the mainstream Broadway theatre, for America had to invent the theatre of its own outside the Broadway. This dramatic form off the Broadway was evolved by a group of young playwrights who were veritably displaced and culturally dislocated. Jerry Tallman, a regular drama critic and who used to write for the non-mainstream art periodical, *Village Voice,* had coined a new term to categorically define the works of these playwrights; he called them "Off Off Broadway". Michael Smith had a point to make when he said: "(These) plays are strikingly American and modern in style, frame of reference and sensibility; they could not have been written anywhere else or at any other time" (13).

Till the first half of the century drama in America has been a provincial extension of the European dramatic tradition. The twentieth century playwrights, therefore, did not have to struggle to invent a new theatrical idiom of their own. Playwrights like Eugene O'Neil, Thornton Wilder, Clifford Odets, Elmer Rice, Maxwell Anderson, Tennessee Williams, Arthur Miller and even Edward Albee, according to Albert Poland and Bruce Mailman, followed a theatrical line originated by Ibsen. Chekov and Strindberg (xii). Robert Brunstein, Dean of Yale Drama School, remarked in 1954:

American drama often seems to be the most mundane form of legitimate culture since eighteenth century sentimental comedy, a form to which it has more than a little resemblance. Our serious drama is informed by a debased Freudianism and our comedies are set in motion by men chasing women. (qtd. in Freedman, 101)

In spite of the significant dramatists produced in America like O'Neil, Miller and others, "America might just as well have been still importing (its) plays from London", wrote William Herman (4). Eventually the production in the Broadway became typical: light comedies, musicals (an indigenous American theatrical form) and the serious plays were mostly with predictable themes like "horror in war", "family is destructive" and psychological explorations.

Writers of the first half of the twentieth century had to invent or revitalise myths to construct a set of symbols for their works. Yeats had to re-establish the whole range of Irish mythology to create symbols for his poetry; Eliot had to draw on the Fisher King phoenix myth to establish 'objective co-relative' for his *The Waste Land*; similarly Ezra Pound was incomprehensible to the 'uninitiated'. But the playwrights belonging to the Off Off Broadway legacy seemed to have been spared of pedantically searching for myths and symbols to construct referential foundations for their works. They, rather, picked on the American folk art and characters that crowded their immediate landscapes. These playwrights invented a group of plays outside the Broadway with enormous variety and distinction, which were characterised by the tenets of new aesthetic poetics, social attitudes an allegiance and which were, observed William Herman, "at odds with the prevailing aesthetics of American theatre, social norms and cultural ideas in force" (10).

The Off Off Broadway playwrights were not a product of a particular institution, nor did they emerge as a group of writers to doggedly follow a well defined agenda or a manifesto. Their status as 'disjunctive temporalities' turned into a common bonding factor for their temperamental unification. Their displacement onto the margin of the cultural space afforded them a commonality of identity and similarities of sensibilities. They had taken recourse to a set of symbols that formed the part of a new syntax. They shared common manifestations syntactically, contextually and theatrically. From a historical perspective, these plays had the unified style that made them similar to than different from each other.

The place of birth of such a powerful and significant art form was the places which, apparently, could be associated with anything but theatre—the cafés and the basement of churches. Café Sino, established in 1958 by one Joe Cino at 31 Cornelia Street in New York, happened to be the first venue to produce a play called *The Apollo Bellac* by Jean Giraudoux in 1967 which, in fact, set off the Off Off Broadway movement in America. This was followed by the Judson Memorial Church's *The Judson Poet's Theatre*, which became the "grand-daddy of the Off Off Broadway theatre movement" (Poland, xx). The two other early centres of the Off Off Broadway activities were Café la Mama, established by energetic and enthusiastic Ellen Stewart who later became the spirited guardian janitor, fund raiser, tour manager, press agent as well as the conceptual leader of the artists that flocked her café. The fourth address of the Off Off Broadway was the Theatre Genesis at St. Mark's Church-in-the-Bowery, founded by Ralph Cook in 1964 to "discover authentic theatre voices and develop them toward a kind of subjective realism", and one of the most significant voices they discovered in the process was that of Sam Shepard who made his debut with *Cowboy Mouth* and *Rock Garden* on 16 October, 1964. From there he emerged, according to Leslie Wade, "the latest great American playwright" (1). These places were small and narrow with non theatrical facilities, makeshift theatres in cellars, bars, lofts, store fronts and coffee houses. Despite the tightness of space, stringent budget, technical limitations, and almost total absence of monetary gain, the playwrights enjoyed enormous freedom, which the vast and huge spaces of the Broadway failed to promise. Finally an alternative location was discovered for drama of a different kind to flourish far away from the Broadway—*Off Off Broadway*.

Earlier the Off Broadway movement produced some of the outstanding theatre figures that had in its list the eminent names like Edward Albee, (his *Zoo Story* was opened with

Beckett's *Krapp's Last Tape* in 1960); Jack Richardson (*The Prodigal*), Jack Gelber (*The Connection*); William Henley (*Mrs. Dally has a Lover*); Arthur Kopit (*Oh Dad, Poor Dad, Mama's Hung You in the Closet and I'm Feelin' So Sad);* William Snyder (*The Days and Nights of Beebee Forster Maker*); Kenneth H. Brown (*The Bug*) and Adrienne Kennedy (*Funny House of a Negro*). But an institution with such a formidable line of eminent playwrights had to make a premature closure forcing the arrival of the Off Off Broadway as an inevitable cultural consequence. Off Broadway discovered itself as not competent enough to take on the practical exigencies. As the movement found a footing, it was eventually beset by the usual troubles-rent hike, unions, rising ticket prices, gradual drop in audience turn out and the growing preoccupation with the 'hit psychology', primarily because even an average Off Broadway production involved quite a considerable amount of financial stake. Off Broadway, inadvertently, became a virtual extension of the Broadway in terms of its management and production pattern. It too followed the Broadway type of 'super productions' with Hollywood cast and exorbitant budget for settings and special effect equipment. Off Broadway productions in the mid-fifties used to cost a few hundred dollars but in the sixties even a regular Off Broadway production would require about $ 10,000 to $ 40,000 as initial investment. As a result, the Off Broadway theatre had to ultimately close down for it was no longer feasible to risk an unconventional or experimental project following their unavoidable commercial vulnerability. The Living Theatre, one of the pioneers of the Off Broadway movement, was finally closed for non payment of tax in October 1963.

Incidentally, it was, in fact, one of the Living Theatre productions that had set forth the aesthetic foundation for the Off Off Broadway theatre movement to sprout. The Living Theatre moved to the Fourteenth Street at Sixth Avenue, and there in 1959 it mounted a production of a new American playwright who cut a work different in idioms and was a radical aberration in its structural form. This was Jack Gelber and the play was *The Connection* under Julian Beck and Judith Melina.

This play was a new experience for the audience. The form was unpretentiously indigenous, the language was starkly contemporary and the style was drastically unconventional. This was staged at the second floor loft with just 160 people as audience and this was what that had created, what Albert Poland later described, a 'forced intimacy' among audience and the artists. The musicians were on stage and they were not locked in a pit and even the audience were made part of the performance unlike the Broadway where the spectators are carefully separated from the proceedings on stage through a curtain representing the fourth wall of the proscenium. With Jack Gelber's *The Connection,* theatre became a ceremony of renewal, for it repositioned drama as a 'folk art'. Critics could no longer afford to ignore the event. Even the mainstream periodical, *Life* magazine, carried out an article on the production. The play set off a new movement in theatre. The Living Theatre had to eventually close down but it left a promise of a new legacy in its wake. It created a new audience and invented the impetus for the new drama and playwrights to arrive. It marked the arrival of the Off Off Broadway.

This movement successfully formed a group of devoted and loyal audience primarily because this new drama betrayed an intense intimacy of experience, for they did not require any extraneous exposure or an orientation to understand the set of symbols and the language used by these playwrights. About this unique intimate dynamics between audience and theatre Michael Smith writes, "They invented it because they were unwanted elsewhere; it invented them because it needed new plays. Neither would exist without the other" (1). The ordinary, everyday America informed the syntax of these plays. To decode the syntax one simply needed to be familiar with the everyday elements that compose the popular sociology of American life—movies, pop corn, cokes, comic strips, cowboys, drugs, rock singers, jazz, Hollywood, TV and other similar objects of American popular culture. Drama, with the arrival of the Off Off Broadway, aesthetically graduated to arrogate into the realm of the postmodern. These plays dealt with the people who were the Andy Warhol of dramatic characters. The characters were picked up from the world of mass media, which formed the body and texture of the twentieth century urban folk art. Off Off Broadway converted pop art into a catalyst to transform art into symbols and it no longer retained as a mere image rather it became a statement of a process where objects transform into adjectives.

The Hollywood movies, America's most formidable 'folk art', are used as cultural references in the Off Off Broadway plays where Hollywood is turned into an adjective to denote excessiveness, opulence, lavishness, sensuality, glamour, high-tech gizmo as well as power. For a sensitive artist like Sam Shepard this was an effortless exercise to dextrously master this art of transforming references of contemporary culture into tangible social symbols; cultural nouns into loaded adjectives. A nation, through this theatre movement, found a means of claiming legitimacy for a cultural experience which has been intimately informing and governing its own identity. Sam Shepard is one of the most successful artists in assigning the immediate cultural reality of the contemporary postmodern America a new dimension. Martin Esslin, the most eminent critic of contemporary drama, has been unambiguous while speaking of the extraordinary importance of Sam Shepard as a dramatist. He emphatically assessed the significance of Sam Shepard and concludes, "Sam Shepard is contemporary American Theatre" (qtd. in McBride, B 2). Shepard's plays are cultural artefacts that critique and document the contemporary cultural history of the country. His aesthetic orientation, remarked Leslie Wade, often signaled wider dislocation in the social and political landscape, for his works speak to an American experience that lies deep within the nation's cultural memory (1997). Shepard, therefore, is always considered as 'the most American' of all the contemporary dramatists of his time. Wynn Handman, director of American Place Theatre, commented, "(Shepard) is like a conduit that digs down into the American soil and what flows out of him is what we're all about" (qtd. in Jack Kroll, 71).

The Americanness of Shepard, like the other Off Off Broadway artists, is constituted by an inherent paradox—he is American by not being an American. He does not represent the civilised or refined America what Paul Berman would call, 'the America of Henry James' (215). Nor is he a 'naturalist' or a mystic' who would write on the American landscape with abundance, impulses and inspiration like that of Walt Whitman. Shepard is, as defined by Berman, a "primitive without peer" (215). He is a "wild rhapsodist, an outsider, a visionary on the edge of American civilisation", says, Leslie Wade. Sam Shepard, the renegade of the Off Off Broadway, became a cult hero of popular culture. Lynda Hart places Shepard as O'Neil's heir apparent and argues that Shepard's "recurrent designation" as America's playwright "should give us a pause" (81), for he has institutionalised a non canonical art.

A major critic of contemporary drama, Leslie A. Wade, in his book, *Sam Shepard and American Theatre* (1980), relates the aesthetic dynamics in Shepard with that of Bakthin's notion of *heteroglossia.* Wade discusses the elements of explosion and disintegration in the plays of Shepard and argues that his plays as well as the venues of the Off Off Broadway movement betrayed a *heteroglossic* expression in terms of their centrifugal impulses that they exuded as parts of an unconventional art form. He points out that the process "manifests itself through irreverence, eruptive expression, unconventional stylistic practices and multiple positioning" (23). This process, in fact, involves a fundamental politics of opposition, which affronts and resists the conservative forces that regulate social conversation, art and artist. Shepard's theatre belongs to the counterculture paradigm that challenged the mainstream cultural codes, contested its narratives, undermined its values and disrupted its modes of production by the sheer anarchy of its *heteroglossic* manifestations. Wade illustrates this chemistry of counterculture in one of the early plays of Shepard, *Icarus's Mother* (1965, produced in Café Cino), where the visceral theatrics and the end-of-the-world scenario appear to negate any form of cohesion or centrism. His plays contest the nation-state consensus and its media representations of the white middle class. *La Turista* (at American Place Theatre on 4

March, 1967) is one of Shepard's another significant productions that formidably illustrate this dramatic characteristic of anti-mainstream complacency. The American Place Theatre was co-founded by Wynn Handman and Reverend Sidney Lanier in 1967 and this was Handman who had remarked of this place as "free from pressures of the market" (vii). It even offered the writers the option to bar critics from the productions and Shepard was one of the first writers to have taken this option with the objective to insulate the artist and his work from being controlled and regulated by the forces of canonical culture. The artistic struggle to achieve this insulation is one of the fundamental themes that a major body of Shepard's work is preoccupied with.

Shepard began his dramatic career in the early sixties, the time that witnessed the arrival of a new generation with an exuberant national spirit, which coincided with John F. Kennedy's becoming of one of the youngest American Presidents (1961-63), one who personified the new generation's idealism and the renewed vigour of nationalism. Kennedy espoused hope, a vision of altruism and sacrifice against the selfish complacency of the consumerist fifties. But the assassination of Kennedy (1963) was a major blow to the edifice of that growing idealism of the young America. This had affected a gradual shift of attitude from what was called "the constricted world view of the Eisenhower era" (1952-60). That was the period the seed of counterculture germinated. Shepard remarked about the time in one of his interviews to Robert Goldberg, "Well, everybody suddenly felt liberated, and the restricted behaviour that was a tradition in this country for years was blown apart" (43). This was also the time when the growing power of corporate America intimidated an uncertain generation, a generation that already expressed their unwillingness to accede to the materialistic morality of their parents, for despite the obvious material prosperity in which the new generation was reared, they looked for an alternative vision, an alternative American dream.

That was the time when Shepard came to New York, which itself was quite a huge cultural revelation for him. He spoke about his experience, "when I go to New York, it was a mixture of being thrilled and awe-struck and scared all at the same time" (qtd. in Goldberg, 43). Shepard later revealed the impact through his plays. He says:

> My plays were influenced by everything happening to me. A lot of them came out of fear and anger, because that's what was going on. There was an extreme kind of street paranoia in those days-the Kennedy trip, Malcom X, and the Panthers. The shit was hitting the fan and everybody had the sense that there was a flood coming. (qtd. in Goldberg, 47)

Shepard also described his New York experience as "like being in a fun park" (qtd. in Chubb 200). As a youth Shepard followed frank hedonism and was engaged in the pursuit of the new and the exciting. His sex life during the time was indiscriminately active and was a hard core patron of drug culture. All those were effective approaches of rejecting values of societal propriety. This rejection was not only reflected in the radical lifestyle of individuals, it was also evidenced in the avant-garde art of the time. Jackson Pollock's abstract expressionism, whom Shepard admired as one of his models; films of Keneth Anger; pop art of Andy Warhol; music of John Cage, Merce Cunnigham and Maya Daren who produced transgressive art in music, dance and other art forms, which were characterised by spontaneity, playfulness and stark originality, influenced Shepard in shaping his sensibilities as an artist. Andy Warhol set up a new norm of claiming artistic value of artwork with his path breaking painting of soup cans. He pioneered a new historical epoch in art history. This was followed by the art of Allan Kaprow and Claes Oldenberg as well as Jim Dine where movement, sculpture, painting and sound were blended into 'non-matrixed' collage events. These champions of avant-garde art of the early sixties reconceptualised art practices and affected forced decentering of aesthetic authorities. Shepard was exposed to a huge exploration of counterculture art activities in New York, which was the epicentre of this movement. Sally Banes, therefore, described New York as the major post World War II world centre of International art (4). Shepard absorbed this aesthetic outlook and expressed them in his work turning his plays into, as Wade puts it, "...bonafide products of counterculture theatre" (12). Shepard began his career as a playwright with two one act plays, *The Rock Garden* and *Cowboy Mouth* (October 10, 1964 at Theatre Genesis), that featured young protagonists of his age who would crudely and emphatically reject the moral universe of parental values and would vehemently reflect the turbulent inner life of the playwright himself beset with an agonising sense of angst.

Sam Shepard was born in 1943. His father, Samuel Shepard Rogers, was in service, took his family from one place to another. After having a short stint at Pasadena he settled with his family in a small town at Duarte, but as Duarte did not offer the facilities of modern living, they shifted once again. This time they shifted to a converted greenhouse in an avocado ranch where Shepard's father proved to be a poor farmer. But the intimacy with soil evoked a sense of belongingness to the mind of young Shepard and this is where he discovered the roots of his language. Much later, in one of his interviews, with Goldberg, Shepard nostalgically recalled:

> To me the biggest tragedy was moving from an agricultural to an urban industrial society. It was a great undertow that demolished the family feelings that were well rooted in America. You know the Ford Motor Company comes out with these little cars that suddenly allow kids who've been harvesting wheat all day to drive off the fuck off the farm to the city. (in Goldberg, 44)

He would ruefully observe, "it's a deeply painful experience finding ourselves in these bodies that are essentially geared toward a rural civilisation. It's as though we've been transported to another planet and didn't know how we got there" (Goldberg, 44). For him it seemed to be a fatal ritual for a forceful *burial of life* leading to a veritable linguistic amnesia of a nation, for Shepard believes, "language comes from the earth" (Goldberg, 44). This traumatic awareness of lost innocence prompted him to write one of his monumental works, *Buried Child* (1978 for which he won his first Pulitzer Prize in 1979). His biographer Ellen Oumano mentions a scene in the Hollywood movie *Days of Heaven* (1978) where Shepard and

Richard Gere were the major casts. Oumano compares Gere with Shepard when both of them gazed across a wheat field. Oumano writes, "accomplished actor as he may be, we know (Gere) is seeing wheat; when we look in Shepard's eyes, something more is going on, he's doing more than acting, perhaps he's writing *Buried Child*" (3).

He married glamorous actress O-Lan Johnson in November 1969 whom he had met at the sets of Cafe La Mama. He had a short romantic stint with a rock poet, Petti Smith, with whom he wrote *Cowboy Mouth* (1971). But he soon recovered from his infatuation and came back to O-Lan from whom he had his first child (son), Jesse Mojo. He finally found gorgeous Jessica Lange who was, like Shepard, from a country background and with whom he could share his own sensibilities. Both were married and both were artists (Jessica was working as an actress opposite Shepard in *Raggedy Man* in 1981 when they first met each other). By 1983 they started living together. From this relationship Hannah and Samuel were born in 1986 and '87 respectively. Shepard now has settled with Jessica in Minnesota to, as Stephen Schift would say, "raise cattle" (84).

As a man with intimate links with family and his social landscape, Shepard became nostalgic when he saw the collapse of this social institution. Shepard's adolescence has been a mixed experience under the strictly disciplinarian and patriarchal attitude of his father who had a sad tale to tell about himself. Shepard explained to *New York Times*, "it was during the depression and my dad was forced to join the army so as to support his mother and younger brothers. As a kid I heard the stories and grew up knowing that my dad really suffered" (qtd. in Oumano 13). His father could not recover from the impact of the 'good war', nor could he recover from his alcoholism and would leave his family many a times until his wife let him to be alone in the desert as the colorful teller of fabulous tales. The impact of Shepard's father haunted him throughout his dramatic career, the shadow of which prominently figured in the character of Travis in *Paris Texas* (the screen play which won the prestigious Palm d'Or at the 1984 Cannes Film Festival). Travis is a wondering father traversing the southwestern desert fueled by the limitless love for his wife, Jane and his son, Hunter. Even Lee and Austin's father in *True West*, and Dodge in *Buried Child* reflected Shepard's memories of his own father. (One of the most moving examples of father-son relationship is between Travis and Hunter in *Paris, Texas*. Hunter's final acceptance of father by imitating him is one of the most powerful moments in the play). His father allowed Shepard to a little Dixieland music on the radio while studying and was allowed to play the drum and eventually he started playing for a rock band, the *Holy Modal Rounders,* which though didn't record much but had a cult fan following. It suited his needs. He became an insider to an alternative lifestyle from where he plucked symbols to construct the syntax for the narrative of his plays. He betrayed a non-traditional texture in his plays which, in terms of Aristotelian parameters, could well be described as anti-plays.

Shepard is a playwright of Jazz and Rock and Roll culture. He used to sit with several free-form Jazz groups which made its impact in the plays of Shepard (the free-from Jazz stuff of Niles, the Jazz musician, would frighten Louis and Pablo in *Suicide in B-Flat*). He would write scores for *Pecos Bill* and *Tooth of Crime*; he would also play the drum for the bands that played for his productions; besides, he developed greater rapport with the musicians than with the other theatre people of his productions. As Oumano observes, music clearly shaped and distinguished both his subject and style. Shepard talked at length about the connection between music and his writing process:

I've practiced Jack Kerouac's discovery of jazz sketching with words ... following the exact principles as a musician does when he's jamming. After periods of this kind of practice, I get the haunting sense that something in me writes but it's not necessarily me. ... This identical experience happened to me once when I was playing with the *Holy Modal Rounders*. (1986: 5)

The narrative of his plays is structured through the manipulation of rhythm, as rhythm is what Shepard considers to be an agent of unification in a work of art because it is what that provides structure as well as form, without which there is no life. In Shepard's family trilogy (*Buried Child, Curse of the Starving Class*, and *True West*) it's the rhythm of familial certainty that collapses leading to the crisis, so too, in the plays like *Tooth of crime, Suicide in B-Flat, Geography of a House Dreamer et al*, where the creativity of the artist is suddenly snapped following the abrupt distortion in the rhythm with which the artists grew up and constituted their respective universes of meaning. Shepard's characters mostly make abortive attempts to retrieve the buried rhythms of life by desperately capturing the nuances of fractured rhythms that accompany them through their bursts of monologues, sudden switching, gearing down to quiet loneliness, and reinstallations of the mythologies. For Shepard word is the 'imagery in motion', when rhythms are the tools to create the inarticulated meanings. Oumano identifies the elements that together formed Shepard, 'the playwright, the musician, the artist, the screenplay writer, the movie star, the cowboy, the family man (1986: 6).

Works Cited

Banes, Sally. *Greenwich Village*. Durham NC: Duke University Press, 1993.

Baudrillard, Jean. *Selected Writings*. Ed. Mark Poster. Cambridge: Polity Press, 1988.

Chubb, Kenneth. "Metaphors, Mad Dogs and Old Time Cow Boys: An Interview with Sam Shepard". Ed. Bonnie Maranca, *American Dream: The Imagination of Sam Shepard*. New York: Performing Arts Journal Publications, 1981.

Feigngold, Michael. *Grove New American Theatre*. New York: Grove Press, 1993.

Freedman, Morris. *American Drama in School Context*. Carbondale: Southern Illinois UP, 1971.

Gilaman, Richard. *Sam Shepard: Seven Plays*. New York: Bantam Books, 1981.

Goldberg, Robert. "Off Off Broadway's Street Cowboy". *Rolling Stone's College Paper*, October, 1994.

Haber, Fern. *Beyond Postmodern Politics: Lyotard, Rorty, Foucault*. New York: Routledge, 1994.

Hart, Lynda. "Sam Shepard's Pornographic Visions" *Studies in Literary Imagination*. 21: 2 (1988).

Herman, William. *Understanding American Drama.* Carolina: University of South Carolina Press, 1987.

Kroll, Jack, constantee Guthrie and Janet Huck. "Who is that tall, dark stranger?" *Newsweek,* 11 November, 1985.

Lyotard, Jean Francois. *Postmodern Condition: A Report on Knowledge.* Tr. Geoff Benington and Brian Masumi. Manchester: Manchester UP, 1984.

McBride, Stuart. "Sam Shepard-Listener and Playwright". *Christian Science Monitor,* 23 December, 1980.

Oumano, Ellen. *Sam Shepard: The Life and Work of American Dreamer.* New York: St. Martin's Press, 1986.

Poland, Albert and Bruce Mailma. "Introduction". *The Off Off Broadway Book: The Plays, People, Theatre.* Indianapolis: The Bobb's Merill Co., 1972.

Rogoff, Gordon. "America Screened". *Village Voice.* 17 December, 1985.

Rosen, Carol. "Emotional Territory: An Interview with Sam Shepard". *Modern Drama,* 36:1 (1993).

Schift, Stephen. "Shepard on Broadway". *New Yorker,* 22 April, 1984.

Shepard, Sam. "Language, Visualisation and the Inner Library". Ed. Bonnie Maranca, *American Dream: The Imagination of Sam Shepard..* New York: Performin Arts Journal Publications, 1981.

_____. *Tooth of Crime.* In *Sam Shepard: Seven Plays.* New York: Bantam Books, 1981.

_____. *Angel City and Other Plays..* New York: Urizen Books, 1977.

_____. *Geography of a Horse Dreamer, Suicide in B-flat, Seduced, Fool for Love and other Plays.* New York: Bantam Books, 1984.

_____. *The Mirror of Production.* Trans. Mark Poster. St. Louis: Telos Press, 1975.

Smith, Michael. "Introduction". Eds. Nick Ozel and Michael Smith. *Eight Plays from Off Off Broadway.* Indianapolis: Bobb's Merill co., 1966.

Wade, Leslie A. *Sam Shepard and the American Theatre.* Westwood: Greenwood Press, 1997.

Wetzsteon, Ross. "The Genius of Sam Shepard". *New York,* 24 November, 1980.

3

Relocating Shepard

Shepard, despite being a dramatist of the fringe, could provoke critical attention from the elite critics. The vivid glow of Shepard's personality seldom went unnoticed. In his essay, "Inside the Words" (*Time Out*, April, 1977), Robert Downey writes, "when he comes into town to work, the props – a clean late model pick up truck with a ventilated straw hat on the dash board, the cloths, somewhere between working rancher in town on business and Ivey League grade student on a very casual country weekend fit the non image .... It's possible to read in his manner some faint traces of the mantrie sensibility, that produced the ironic characters in the plays, the kind of look you see in reformed alcoholics, returned Viet Nam Veterans, ex-speed freaks – possible, but neither easy nor certain (11)."

Shepard could finally obtain an institutional recognition by winning the Pulitzer Prize in 1979 for his *Buried Child* (1978) even before having any play of his ever staged at the Broadway. In 1980 Ross Wetzsteon writes, "Shepard, now 37, is the greatest American playwright of his generation" (*NewYork*, Nov. 24, p. 20). Wetzsteon goes on to write, "(Shepard) is not only the most inventive in language and revolutionary in craft. Shepard is the writer whose work most accurately maps the interior landscape of his society. And his life is as quintessentially American as his work is (20)."

Patti Smith, the rock poet with whom Shepard had a short romantic stint, devotes a poem to Shepard to highlight his radical personality:

> He was bad
> la – lu – lud
> a drunken kid
> He yodelled like a cowboy rolling
> And sliding
> All over them by dinosaur
>
> People started up at him, he didn't care
> He was a renegade with nasty habits
> He was screech owl
> He was a man plying cowboys
> ['Sam Shepard' in *Nine Random Years (7+2)*
> qtd. in Jasbir Jain, 91]

Rick Foster, however, while commenting on the critical responses to Shepard's works, is quite critical about the inadequate critical attention Shepard received. He accuses that most critics having been only too keen to focus on the exotic sites of images, ritual and other aspects in Shepard's plays. They were more interested to reduce his plays into meaning, as if drama cannot exist beyond the realms of common understanding. He argues that the "political economy of the dramatic region of (Shepard) is not probed." He writes, "At best these critics are to Shepard what the *National Geographic* Magazine is to Guatemala" (51).

Blurbs on the books pertaining to Shepard describe him as the most brilliant and irreverent young playwright of America. Ronald Heyman describes Shepard as "a poet of the theatre" (163). "Sam Shepard is phenomenal "Much of Shepard's work is unforgettable, seen or read once", writes Stanley Kauffman (66). Critics like Michel J. Hayes describes Shepard as the "rock star of American theatre" (132). The media characterised Shepard as a more "machoist" personality by describing him as "theatre's version of Clint Eastwood" who, like the movie image of Clint Eastwood, was projected as the high plains drifter who did not take the beaten path of the Broadway, but instead blazed a trail elsewhere (Ann. C. Hall 19). Some critics coined a more rococo appelation for Shepard, "bucking bronco of American theatre" (Richard Gilman ix). Richard Gilman provided a memorable term that became a favourite for the Shepard critics—'Shaman'. He wrote, "Sam Shepard is a

Shaman—a New World Shaman ... Sam is as American as coyote magic mushroom, Rock 'n' Roll and medicine bundles" (2). Martin Esslin provided a sort of finality to the ongoing exercise of defining Sam Shepard when he said, "Sam Shepard is contemporary American theatre" (qtd. in Gilman 2).

Despite being a playwright of the margin, Sam Shepard is so significantly visible that his presence is difficult to ignore, primarily because he deftly penetrates the very essence of Americanness. He simply speaks of America in American idioms. He thinks penetratingly about current conditions in America and he thinks in theatrical terms, writes Hayes. Shepard's creative source has been his own surroundings of his small town experience in the towns like Azusa and Duarte. He centred the action of his play, *The Unseen Hand* (1970), on the abandoned wreck of a 1958 Chevrolet, amidst the garbage of empty tin cans, Coca-Cola bottles and other urban dross. Even the setting for the play, *The Mad Dog Blues* (1971), is also predominantly composed by similar images.

Shepard situates his protagonist against a typical American backdrop which is either clustered with the images of corporate refuse or with the wide expanses of the West – a recurrent theme in American landscape. He is a comfortable interpreter of events and individuals located in such quintessentially American sites – the West, Hollywood, suburban driveways, the hotel rooms. Against such a familiar backdrop Shepard deals with the characters who are so typically American.

Shepard's plays have been produced in the European countries like England, Germany, Austria and Switzerland since 1968. In Germany alone as much as 55 separate productions of his 15 plays were performed in German till 1991. The reception of his plays in Europe has been mixed. Carol Benet observes in *Sam Shepard on the German Stage* (1993), "Shepard's scripts presented not only language problems but conceptual one as well" (6). Benet points out that Shepard speaks to an American audience in a colloquial form of the English language. Through language, writes Benet, Shepard evokes certain stereotypical images of America and the people who inhabit it. That is, the intimacy of Shepard with his cultural grammar makes his plays profoundly American, and to understand his plays one must know what America is all about.

Shepard, quite unassumingly exposes the inner vulnerabilities of the seemingly invincible heroes of popular culture of America by lifting the carapace of their solidity through his candid theatrical admissions. Shepard's significance lies not in his mere depiction of an American reality in stark terms, but in his ability to enable theatre to emerge as one of the most powerful ideological discourses to achieve a rare distinction to redefine the fundamentals of a nation's cultural dream. Sam Shepard has opened up a new cultural debate on the validity of artistic creations in the given circumstances of postmodern condition. Shepard is unsympathetic in disclosing the bare realities that beset an artist. He is critical about the entire mechanism and procedure through which artists are heuristically produced by the market.

Shepard is a product of the time when the occluded boundaries of culture collapse causing, as said by Frederick Jameson in his essay, "Postmodernity and Consumer Society"—the effacement of boundaries between the high culture and mass or commercial culture. It is a time when the teleological view of history is displaced following the abandonment of canonical narrative by the new generation. The time witnesses the emphasis on 'discontinuity' and 'open-unfinished qualities'; it tries to explore the new territories of history by rediscovering the myths, symbols and the shared assumptions of the community that remained unattested by the established institutions of conventional disciplines. The breakdown of cultural boundaries is characterised by the formation of a new narrative in every aspect of art comprising discontinuous images, simulacra and floating signifiers (Leonard Wilcox, 560). Culture assumes new signification as the mass of commercial culture gains a new legitimacy following progressive termination of modernist elitism.

Shepard's plays capture this quintessential transitional tension of the new cultural poetics. He has not come out from a precise theatrical tradition, but as Gilman puts it, from the breakdown or absence of it (xi). The apparent absence of any profound American dramatic tradition made Shepard somewhat dismissive about a career in drama. He said in 1971, "I don't want to be a playwright, I want to be Rock 'n'Roll star .... I got into writing plays because I had nothing else to do. So I started writing to keep from going off the deep end" (qtd. in Gelber 3).

Shepard's shift to drama is marked by the accompanying theatrical idioms that characterise his works. Music is a dominant aspect in Shepard's plays. For him, "A play is like music – ephemeral, elusive, appearing and disappearing all the time. No one ever left a Rolling Stone concert confused" (qtd. in Gelber). He tries to find out a way to actually have music become an actor by allowing music take part in the drama the same way as language does. Shepard's narrative, in rejecting a conventional intellectual form, is more akin to, as Shepard himself notes, Jackson Pollock and the Rolling Stones. Shepard has used the structure of music of Jazz improvisation because for him, as Bonnie Maranca points out, Jazz is more than a structural composition. Music as an approach to composition embodies an attitude that is at the heart of Shepard's work: spontaneity of expression. Not chance but improvisation (qtd. in Gelber, 30). Shepard brings in the familiar figures of popular culture and cultural myths, but they are exposed theatrically through unfamiliar methods. The plays structurally look disjointed and elliptical because, as Gelber puts it, "he has abandoned the conventions of coherence and has attempted to create a theatre in which emotional, psychological, or spiritual states are presented directly to the audience" (7). Through his plays Shepard attempts to explore what he himself has defined as "emotional territory" (qtd. in Rosen, 1993).

Technically, Shepard spreads his dramatic action across a space that is emotional rather than physical. As in *Angel City, Seduced, Suicide in B-flat.* The space, therefore, becomes alien to the audience in the first encounter till they make a tacit agreement to enter the inner territory of the characters.

In Shepard, time is immediate rather than sequential, as time is associated with the mind of the characters and they are placed outside the chronologically informed temporal framework. This is a key element in Shepard's plays like *Melodrama Play, Angel City, The Mad Dog Blues, Suicide in B-Flat, Fool for Love* where characters are oblivious of a dual time frame as they live exclusively within the limitations of their own temporal confines. As in *Seduced,* physical time could not deter Henry Heckamore from going back to his olden days to establish a contact with the girl friends of his earlier times.

Characters in Shepard are spontaneous rather than coherent. Like the storyline itself, the characters too are fragmented, impulsive, incoherent who are prone to abrupt shift, hence, they become unpredictable and wayward and are immune to any readily definable category. Shepard believes, "personality is everything that is false in a human being. Social individuality is divorced from humanity" (qtd. in Gelber 8).

His story focuses on consciousness rather than on behaviour. Gelber explained the mode by pointing out at the frequent fragmentation of the storyline, abrupt shift of focus, even a seemingly secondary character assumes centrality and the hero disappears from stage. These elements reflect the continuity of consciousness rather than the continuity of behaviour. Niles in *Suicide* for a considerable period of time remains absent as the play focuses on the role of Pablo, Louis, Petrone and Paulette who desperately look for a meaningful space in their own respective ways to contextualise their position. This is how Shepard creates new dramatic vision of space, time, character and story.

In dealing with the crisis of the artist, Shepard is intimately self reflexive. Through this theme he often comes back to himself. Shepard was in the forefront of the generation that fought for "Eros" like the counterculture intellectual, Herbert Mercuse, the author of *Eros and Civilisation* (1974), would mention.

Shepard grew up amidst the appraisal of a new youthful idealism following the apocalyptic disaster of the Vietnam War (1974-75). The war marked a defining moment in US history, triggering a struggle between authority and dissent, which also led to an interrogation of the value and viability of a nationalist culture. This in-built mentality of protest was also one of the basic tenets of the Rock movement of the sixties and the late seventies. They sounded an annulment of an overarching system of cultural totalitarianism. Shepard takes up this issue along with the fact of the artist's entrapment within that system.

As an artist, Shepard had to undergo the usual upheavals on the economic front as his was an essentially anarchic, unsystematic enterprise. Funding and patronage was uncertain, which led to an uneasy working condition. As he drew more attention as a playwright, he started getting honours and rewards. Shepard initially prohibited any review of his play *La Turista* (1967), yet Elizabeth Hardwick saw the play and wrote a glowing review in *New York Review of Books* (1967). Shepard, meanwhile, received a grant from the Yale University to explore relations between experimental writing and the TV/ Film industry. In 1967 he was honoured with the prestigious Rockefeller Grant. Thus, despite being a non-conformist artist, Shepard is trapped by the interpellating distinctions of cultural recognitions.

During his early years, Shepard got himself engaged in some odd jobs. He used to work as a low paid employee in places like Hickory House Restaurant, The village Gate Jazz Club and Marie's Crisis Cafè. But with the money he received as grants and honours he could engage himself as a full time writer. Robert Coe writes that this was the time which was the "beginning of the end" of "Shepard's enchantment with Off Off Broadway" (120). In the *Theatre Mailbag* section of the the *New York Times* a reader, one Wynn Handman, wrote:

"When *La Turista* was first published at the American Place, Shepard decided against inviting the critics. He didn't want anyone connected with the creation of the production feel the pressure of success or failure based on the critic's opinion. He watched the audience every night ... Now in 1977, the general press, the public and resident regional theatres are more respective to a new play by Sam Shepard. American playwrights may be finding greater acceptance." (*The New York Times,* Sunday, March 20, 1977, 28).

This acceptance is both absorption and legitimation, which is immediately followed by expectations forcing the artist move towards the ambivalent arena of doubt and apprehension of fame. Through this process the artist gradually approximates the institutions of legitimate cultural agencies, and art no longer remains a vehicle for self-expression or lucid diversion, as Cody in *Geography* announces: "at first it's all instinct. Now it's work" (94). Theatre for Shepard too became a job.

Shepard makes a close survey of the artists who are trapped in a cultural mesh with which he is quite familiar. He, therefore, could make an authentic representation of the artists who reflect the similar trauma of their creative self like their own creator (Shepard). They become the objective correlatives of Shepard's own self. This is why the plays of Shepard are so authentic, unpretentious and immediate which can easily capture the American imagination of which his plays are themselves a product.

The forthcoming chapter would look in details at the plays that reflect Shepard's recurring concern with the position of an artist and the problematic of his creation. Shepard's artist is not the proverbial superman with divine power. He is rather a part of the common culture and is constantly denied existence beyond the realm of the demarcated territory as an autonomous entity. The study will examine the process through which the artist is produced, translocated and the methodologies that eventually subjugate him. The study would also examine whether there is any possibility of artistic redemption for a creator in Shepard's work.

Works Cited

Downey, Robert. "Inside the Words". *Time Out*, April, 1977.

Benet, Carol. *Sam Shepard on the German Stage: Critics, Politics, Myths.* New York, Frankfurt am Main: Peter Lang Publishing Inc., 1993.

Foster, Rick. Sam Shepard: Art is made out of argument with ourselves. n.d.

Gilman, Richard. "Introduction". *Sam Shepard: Seven Plays.* New York: Bantam Books, 1981.

Hall, Ann C. "Fire in the Snow Shepard's Female Saviors." *Theatre Criticism.* Ed. Stanley Kauffman. New York: Performing Arts Journal Publications, 1983.

Hall, Ann C. "Fire in the Snow Shepard's Female Saviors." *A Kind of Alaska: Women in the Plays of O'Neil, Pinter and Shepard.* Carbondale: Southern Illinois UP, 1993.

Hayes, Michael J. "Sam Shepard". *American Drama.* Ed. Clive Bloom. Kentucky: Macmillan, 1995.

Heyman, Ronlad. *Theatre and Anti-Theatre: Movements since Beckett.* New York: Oxford UP, 1979.

Jain, Jasbir. "The West and the Plays of Sam Shepard". *Literature and Popular Culture: A Festschrift for Isaac Sequira.* Eds. R.S. Sharma, Sukhbir Singh *et al.* Hyderabad: Cauvery Publications, 1983.

Jameson, Frederick. "Postmodernism and Consumer Society". *The Anti-Aesthetic: Essays on Postmodern Culture.* Ed. Hall Foster. Port Townsend, 1983.

Wetzsteon, Ross. "The Genius of Sam Shepard". *New York,* 24 Nov.

_____. "Ioduction". *Fool for Love and Other Plays by Sam Shepard.* New York: Bantam Books, 1984.

Wilcox, Leonard. "Modernism vs. Postmodernism: Shepard's *Tooth of Crime* and the Discourse of Popular Culture". *Modern Drama.* Downsview ON Canada: 30:4 (1987).

4

Arresting Cowboy in a Godless Meadow: Artists as Surrogate Creators

Artist in Shepard finds himself as an uneasy insider to a cultural landscape which for him appears to be a space of 'unfreedom'. Shepard has been a sensitive respondent to the subjugating cultural politics of the new order that encompasses every aspect of an artist's creative existence. This is the zone of conflict that the artist is translocated into from his traditional milieu of freedom. Shepard's deep concern with this dislocation of the artist and his art finds constant resonance in a significant number of his plays. The perennial question of artistic freedom is addressed in the plays like *Melodrama Play* (1967), *Cowboy Mouth* (1971), *The Mad dog Blues* (1971) and *Geography of a Horse Dreamer* (1974) where the artist protagonists are engaged in a futile struggle by default for an escape route from the state of their cultural incarceration. The artist not only struggles against his physical subjugation, he also confronts cultural disorientation of his own prehistory following the disruption of his identity, cultural meanings and myths.

Economic and cultural over-exposure in America has introduced a sense of uncertainty for the nation's historical validity and individual's cultural identity affecting its sense of totality. American landscape and language also, under such circumstances, undergo a process of metamorphosis from, what Shepard calls, the agrarian rural background to the alienating urban space. Shepard, in one of his interviews with Robert Goldberg says: "to me one of the biggest tragedies was moving from an agricultural to an urban industrial society at the turn of the century" (44). This cultural translocation from the rural to the urban is a painful experience for Shepard. It is "like being transported to another planet and did not know how to get there" (44).

Shepard, therefore, makes his artist-protagonists involved with the perennial struggle to construct his own mythological universe through the narrative of reachable memory which, in fact, continues to elude him because even the myths, in post war America, "in its truest form has been demolished" (qtd. in Carol Rosen 5:1993). For Shepard, the exercise of reconstructing an identifiable mythic universe is acutely problematised as it turns out to be a conscious exercise of approximating an illusion because of the artists' awareness that "there is the myth (only) in the sense of a lie" (qtd. in Carol Rosen ibid). Myth is reduced into a part of a historical fantasy that has lost the purpose through which the subject could reach a universe of meaning.

Melodrama Play (1967), first produced at Café La Ma Ma on May 18, 1967, reflects on the changes of meaning in American cultural landscape. This is the first play where Shepard has used rock music and a rock star as the central character. Here Shepard makes a sardonic comment on the process that reduces an artist into a commodity for mass consumption.

In the play Duke Dungens, a rock and roll singer, achieves instant fame because of his hit song: "Prisoners Get Up of Your Homemade Bed." He soon draws attention of the music industry and the academia. Dr. Daniel Damon, a sociologist from Corning University, tries to make him a subject to study how an artist's social environment is affected by his public acclaim. Duke dismisses the professor's academic suit. He broadsides, "Sociologists are movers. They don't hang around waiting for replies. They make up their own if they don't get them on time. And I'd hate to see him do that. To create a lie out of my negligence (*MP* 119)."

Though he can escape the imposition of academy, he fails to escape the tentacles of the music industry.

Duke has been requested by Floyd, the mobster manager, to write another hit song for the forthcoming Phoenix Concert. But as Duke discloses that Drake Dungens is the original creator of his hit song, he was subjected to physical insult. Floyd immediately turns to Drake to sing for him and he does not care that he slugged Duke to death as soon as he became useless for him. This indignified existence of artist reveals the morbid reality of the music industry governed by the whims of the market. The stage setting features two huge black and white posters of Bob Dylan and Robert Goulet with their eyes blinded as *mise-en-scene* which is reflective of the reality of stardom that empties the artist of his identity and creative vision.

The artist is made into a faceless entity within the world of media hegemony. He is appropriated and enslaved by the 'industry' for its corporate interest and he is not allowed to utter anything that does not fall in their scheme of things. Duke's song reveals the artistic predicaments:

> You could not say out loud what we already know
> You should say it is to yourself
> You should keep it in your mouth
> ....
> Nobody knows when the pain got started
> It's still the same as it always was.
>
> (*MP* 116-117)

Artist is subjected to an ordering mechanism where the categories of boundaries, allocations, classifications and other stratifications are well legislated and well defined into existence. This ordering involves the rationalising logic that aims at manipulating everything for its own interest. In the play, *Melodrama Play*, Floyd and Dona are concerned with the next musical 'production' of Duke which must have the ingredients of success: beautiful tune, protest message, poetry so that they can 'sell' it ("when will Duke produce for us his next hit tune ... a shiny new tune that we can sell", 120). Drake finally appropriates his new role and proceeds to make a song for Floyd:

> Drake: Just let me sing a song Peter. Please.
> Let me make up a song for Floyd.
> Peter: That will save your skin but how about mine?
> (*MP* 141)

The issues of artistic freedom, his creativity and exclusivity turn out to be plausible myths because the artist here is not certain even of his own identity. In the play the characters are confused about the identities of each other. Anybody can pretend to be Duke Dungens and anybody can be an imposter of an artist. Even Duke Dungens himself pretends to be Duke Dungens and the confusion is so extreme that Drake and Cisco even turn into one another. Authenticity of creation too becomes an irrelevant issue in the system as finally it is Duke whose interview is broadcast over radio by Dan Damon whose main purpose is to turn the artist into an academic subject rather than discovering the artist in him.

Shepard wrote this play when he himself was gradually exposed to the operations of the art world. He was frequently playing the drum for Holy Modal Rounders, collaborated with Michelangelo Antonioni to write the screenplay, *Zabriskie Point*; and he started dealing with universities, foundations, record companies, movie studios and theatre entrepreneurs that eventually enhanced his antipathy to the system.

II

He himself felt to have been a captive inside a prison like that of Duke Dungens. Shepard too, like his artists, looks for an escape. Shepard got romantically involved with an attractive rock poet / singer, Petti Smith, that jeopardised his three year old marriage with O Lan Johnson. He, however, makes an escape at the Chelsea Hotel where he dramatises his artistic and emotional ambivalence in the play, *Cowboy Mouth* (1971). He wrote the play with Petti Smith pushing the type writer back and forth between them. He invents another rock artist as the protagonist who finds himself in "a reptile heap of dogshit situation" (*CM* 147). The play was first produced at the Traverse Theatre, Edinburgh, on April 12, 1971. The artist Slim in *CM*, like Dungens, is also a prisoner here. But when

Dungens was imprisoned by media operators, Slim is imprisoned by a desperate youngster who has lost her all connections to history, faith and myths. When Dungens was forced to produce songs for the market, Slim was to create songs to reinvent the fictions of myths. Cavale, the kidnapper, wants Slim to emerge as the "Rock 'n' roll Jesus with a Cowboy Mouth" (*CM* 157).

The Cowboy is one of the greatest mythological figures of American culture who enjoys a status, "somewhere above the president and below Christ" (William W. Savage Jr. 154:1975). With the myth of the cowboy two important factors are intrinsically related: that of the wild West and the cult of individual propriety. The cowboy belongs to specific geographic location—the wild west—which symbolises the ethos of savagery, primitivism, promise, wealth and justification to accomplish the task of enlightening the dark world—one of the spiritual duties attached to the 'white men's burden'. He is not only a fictional purveyor of instant justice, but also a cult figure of romantic history. He is the physical reckoner of the possibility of living in the plausible world of the American Dream. As a symbol or myth, the cowboy has transcended all boundaries of limitations. He is not a mere pastoral figure that represents innocence and spiritual purity like that of the Biblical Shepards, the cowboy is a reference to a glorified past. He is also a reflector of one of the characteristics of American cultures that of the deification of an individual and the absence of a community identity. The cowboy is made to pose as the grandest of all individuals. The state of disequilibrium prevalent in the postmodern epoch has made it imperative for individuals to explore the possibilities of regenerating the myths.

The cowboy is, in the context of American culture, a symbol which can be defined, borrowing a term from Raymond Williams, as a means of a "specific communication" (60). The cowboy becomes an artist's reference for the discovery of certain values and its communications. Shepard's self conscious artists are engaged in an act of conceiving a cultural nostalgia which has been a part of the artist's perception of the genetic structures of his sociology—the collective identity. But the artist here is adequately distanced from the romantic West and, instead, he is located in a complicated space of a capitalist market society. Lucien Goldman says that in capitalist society the existence and development of an economic sector has precisely a tendency for disappearance or, at least, a reduction in the status of the collective consciousness (167).

The cowboy happens to enact the role of a messiah in the obvious absence of a spiritual icon, culturally identifiable by the collective American consciousness. He is an allegory of the fast receding American morality. He symbolises, as observed by William W. Savage Jr., truth, chivalry, honesty, courage, loyalty, precision, and other similar virtues. But the present dominance of the corporate economy has reduced them into mere components of marketable '*feuilleton*' (Walter Benjamin).[1] Against this backdrop of the spiritual absence in the technology based repressive social order, the cowboy emerges as a cultural event to allow an ideal continuity of a value-added history for the emplacement of an artist in a virtual discourse of teleological narrative. Because of the artist's supposed capacity for initiating rituals to this direction of cultural salvation, Cavale, in *Cowboy Mouth,* kidnaps Slim.

Shepard, in his search for an American genealogy of myth and the continuity of this emotional narrative, re-creates a hero combining the qualities of two American cult figures – the rock 'n' roll star with the 'cowboy' attitude.

The play, *Cowboy Mouth* (1972),[2] is about a quest for a new messiah, about the creation of new God as the collective repudiation of the old God has become a cultural imperative because "The old God is too far away. He don't represent our pain, no more" (says Cavale in *CM*,156). This defiance of God is necessitated by the realisation of being in a world of complex semantic configurations as against the apparent historical fixities, which again is a construction based on, as Foucault would say "profound intentions and immutable necessities" (157) of the dominant forces. The new God now has to reflect a new image, i.e; "created from... own image" (*CM* 156). Now Cavale stipulates the process of recreating myth to be strictly followed by the abducted artist, Slim, who can't follow his own paradigm of artistic creation like Cody, who is kidnapped to dream the winning number of dogs in *Geography of a House Dreamer*. Cavale too stipulates the process as to how Slim should create his own art: "You gotta collect it. You gotta reach out and grab all the little broken busted up pieces of people's frustration. That stuff in them that is looking for a way out or way in. You know what I mean? The stuff in them that makes them wanna see God's face. And then you gotta take all that into yourself and pour back out. Give it back to them bigger than life. You gotta be unselfish. Like God was selfish. He kept himself hid. He wasn't a performer, man. You gotta be like a rock 'n' roll Jesus with a Cowboy Mouth" (*CM* 156-157).

The artist here like Dungens in *Melodrama Play* is transported to another universe of oppressive discourse where he is exposed to a new series of codes within which he is to create. He is to emerge as a new Saviour to give salvation along the parameters of prescribed norms. He is to deliver even more than God, like a 'real cowboy'. He has to embody all the mythic qualities that have been attributed to the legendary heroes. He is to emerge, like the cowboy, as an archetypal figure of the American dream. Not a mere fictive cowboy, seen in movies and fictions, but rather idealised and mythic; instead of being a 'formula cowboy' he is to turn into an ambiguous cowboy (Mark Siegel 238/9:1982). The cowboy, *vis-à-vis* the artist, turns out to be a means through whom an attempted approximation towards an invented prehistory is made. He is to climb inside America's collective consciousness and evolve a theatrical language and a mythological genealogy that, as David J. De Rose observes, "speaks to America about America" (51-52:1992).

Cavale reveals the quintessential American desperation and almost tragic compulsion to invent a hero, a saviour, in order to keep their dream, their hopes alive. When Slim collapses following excessive violence that he has been subjected to, Cavale realises that it is "her dream (that is) being busted and not his" (*CM* 157). She then articulates her desperation: "My only dream. I spread my dream at your feet, everything I believe in, and you tread all over them with your simply horseshit. Fuck you. Fuck you. Poor, poor baby. I take your world and shake it. Well, you took my fantasy and shit on it. I was doing the streets looking for a man with nothing so I could give him everything. ...And its settled I can't do nothing to alter it. I can't do shit. I can't give you nothing. I can't. I can't. You won't let me". (*CM* 157)

The artist is to emerge as a healer by inducting a faith, for collective self deception, by way of a pretentious demystification of a cultural reassurance. But as Slim discovers the bucolic nostalgia he hears the sound of the river in the traffic noise, his expression and experience when become a reassurance to Cavale:

> Listen to the traffic. It sounds like a river I love rivers... They make up their own paths. New Paths. I tried to make a dam once in a river. I was really proud. I'd stopped a river.... Then it started to rain...all night long it rained. The next morning I ran down to the river, and dam was all busted to shit. ..I never built dam again (158).

Slim's pastoral roots and his intimacy with the sovereign space of nature empower him with a creative gift what Cavale lacks due to the absence of an intimate past. She implores: "I wish I woulda' know you when I was little ... I wish you were around them. I bet you woulda' protected me." (158)

Slim is not a mere artist but he is a hero for Cavale who could assure her a respectable position because he was the one, believes Cavale, who has the ability and strength to protect her. In the world of capitalist aesthetics only "pretty people" have a rightful place. She would recall her experience in one of the school plays. She had "dumb eye patch" and a defective foot for which she had to use metal plates to correct her "duck foot" and she was given the role of an ugly duckling. She agreed to take the role of an ugly duckling because she was made to believe that in the end she would be the pretty swan.

She tells the incident vindictively:

> But you know what they did, Slim? At the end of the play I had to kneel on the stage and cover my head with black shawl and this real pretty blonde-haired girl dressed in a white ballet dress rose up behind me as the swan. I paid all the dues and up rose

> Ballerina Catty like the North Star. And afterwards all the parents could talk about was how pretty she looked ... . I wish you were around then. I bet you woulda' protected me. (158)

She believes Slim to be the cowboy of her dream. "The Cowboy", a pastoral figure, writes Savage Jr, "exists in a primordial state and may, accordingly simply, destroy his antagonists if he cannot intimidate them into submission" (157). He writes: "We in civilised societies are unable to attain this resoluteness of maintaining order, as we do, through systems of intermediaries. But we wear cowboy hats and cowboy boots, and we pretend. Great number of us buy guns, and that is where the pretense ends and the potential begins" (157 ibid).[3]

In order to ascertain a protective carapace around, the new generation voluntarily repudiates the fictionalilty of their heroes and consciously takes them as part of reality. They would not question their authenticity, instead they would "like to know (his) hopes, his aspirations" (*CM* 161).

This desperate cultural preference for fictive figures is an effect of a deep sense of historical provisionality, and as Savage Jr. would observe, "as a young country, with a simultaneous growth of her physical and technological change, America has not developed or had no time to develop, a culture of genuine substance. In comparison to much of the rest of the world, America has only a small shelf of myths" (159). These myths, though may not supplant history, yet it performs a vital function in shaping a social understanding. Hence, Shepard proclaims, that what America needs is a "renaissance of myth" through which "(he) seeks authentic values to sustain the performing self. These values rest in the ability to trust in the imagination and the heart as a repository of emotional truth, the living myth of the past and the present" (qtd. in Robert Coe 65).

History assumes a peculiar onward direction in Shepard's plays. History is somewhat like a dream. Here it is not a mere recollection of the past. It is a kind of what Linda Hart calls, 'historiographic metafiction' [4] (qtd. in John M. Durvell, 562: 1999) where history is to experience a new process of accumulation. Cavale explains:

> "A dream, I'm playing... You don't talk about yesterday stuff. Yah, you fucking coyote, Slim always howling after yesterday. Raymond (the Crow) don't squawk 'bout his old nests. Do you baby ? He sleeps on my belly 'cause my belly's today. Yesterday, yesterday, that's you, sulking shit face-Mr. Yesterday. (*CM* 148).

Robert Coe considers the real meaning of the word 'history" in terms of its Greek root, *istorin* meaning 'to go' find out for yourself (66, ibid). This is, indeed, what Kosmo, Yahoodi, Mae West and others did in *The Mad Dog Blues*—a Hegelian search for the self realisation of human spirit through history. For Hegel, "history is a rational expression of human freedom-the development of spirit in time" (qtd. in Ramon Selden 420). Particular events and physical reality in general are part of a large 'absolute spirit of history'. History therefore is not a mere retrogressive construction towards the confines of 'yesterday', it is rather a ritual of envisaging a dialectical view of the past that underlines change and development. This is an onward peregrination in search for the inner significations of the subject's cultural context. Shepard's subject is eternally enshrouded by an all encompassing universe of mystery. Despite having made desperate attempts to recontextualise the subjective existence, as Elizabeth Proctor proclaims, reality, identity and the ontology of meaning continue to remain eternally elusive (39).[5] Shepard himself has insisted that "By myth I mean a sense of mystery and not necessarily a traditional formula. Character for me is a composite of different mysteries. He's an unknown quantity. If he wasn't, it would be like coloring in the numbered spaces' ("Inner Library", in Maranca, 55:1981).

Through this mysterious power of individual ability, Cavale turns the numb Lobsterman into a rock and roll star through whom Cavale moves to fulfil her needs. She asks through her song –an incantation of sort –to infuse strength and revitalise dry force of man:

> Show me the way to it
> You know I need a friend
> A song to pull me from the hole I'm in
> Give me something low down

> Give me something high
> Pulling in the power of dark or light
> To destroy to the left
> Create on to the right
> Oh come right here
>
> (*CM* 163)

Slim as an artist fails to attain a historical space for autonomous existence. His survival is a necessary construction by his audience, his abductors. It is not he who enjoys the power but it's the audience who holds the key to make or unmake the artist. As singer Cher, celebrated pop diva, has put it, "They raise the heroes to make them fall."

The artist does not exist as an authentic social entity. He lives as a myth that they search for. The very act of searching for a mythology is an assertion of its absence. But in case of Shepard's characters it is also an act of translocation of the self into the realm of fantasy and illusion about the past. Shepard writes of New England activism, "New England is festering with bi-centennial madness, as though desperately trying to resurrect the past to reassure ourselves that we sprang from somewhere. A feeling that in the past at least there was some form of structure and that our present state of madness could be healed somehow by ghosts. Everywhere replicas of history are being sold" (*Rolling Thunder Logbook* 45).

Slim, aware of his proto-historicity as an artist, is to undergo the torture of being severed from the connections with his quasi-historical past and yet he attempts to manufacture ideal dreams for his abductor. Slim complains:

> I've a baby! My own baby! With its own cradle! You've stolen me away from my baby's cradle! You've put a curse on me! I have a wife and a life of my own ! Why don't you let me go! I am not no rock 'n' roll star. That's your fantasy. You've kept me cooped up here for how long has it been now? I've lost track of the time. A long time. A long fucking time. And I'm still not a star! (*CM* 154).

The process of creativity, on the other hand, is redefined by Cavale with new paradigms. Cavale substantiates the process of artistic creation as an 'esçape' (165). She justifies:

> People want a street angel. They want a saint but with a cowboy mouth. Somebody to get off on when they can't get off on themselves. I think that's what Mick Jagger is trying to do... What Bob Dylan seemed to be for a while. A sort of God in our image... y'a know? Mick Jagger came close but he got too conscious. For a while he gave me hope... but he misses. He is not whole (156).

The artist, however, fails to emerge as an authentic manifestation of the fantasised myths because he himself turns out to be a product of, as in the case of Slim, competing as well as incompatible desires of a desperate community orphaned by the absence of a God, hence, Cavale and other posit:

> Any great mother fucker rock 'n' roll song can rise me... higher than all of Revelations. We created rock 'n' roll from our own image, its our child... a child that gotta burst in the mouth of saviour" and this new Jesus is to arrive in Yeatsian fashion, "the rock 'n' roll star in his highest state of grace will be the new saviour... rocking to Bethlehem to be born (*CM* 156).

Myth for Shepard is a powerful means of reaching out to the mystified territory of the self. The absence of myth is an agonising reality for the playwright "because (myth) takes to the emotions and not to the end. It moves us into an area of mystery." (*RTL* 62). For Shepard some myths are "poisonous to believe, but others have the capacity for changing something for a minute or two." (*RTL* 62). Shepard is aware of the replacement of myth with the quintessential fantasy of the American dream. But he finds that myth has the capacity, which fantasy does not, to serve people to connect themselves in time to the past and "thereby connect themselves to the present and the future" (qtd. in Rosen 5:1993) as well. For Shepard, "Myth is so powerful and so strong that it acted as a thread in culture" (Rosen 5:1993). But such a powerful means of approximating culture's prehistory is 'demolished' easily and what is left, points out Shepard, is "only the fantasies about it" (qtd. in Rosen 5:1993). The myths even have ceased to speak, and articulate the inner self. Shepard says, "they speak to nations about the past. But they don't connect with anything. We've lost touch with the essence of myth." (in Rosen 5:1993)

The protagonists in Shepard at times try to connect themselves with a supposed substance of history but which turns out to be a 'fruitless' exercise. Shepard himself is aware of the tempered and provisional enunciation of the characters who are engaged in search of a connection, a sense of belongingness. In their desperate bid to find out a connection, the characters construct themselves into mythic heroes, existing on the fragile foundation of, what Shepard says, "made up information" (*RTL* 76) but it seems to be of little consequence because America "still wants to believe it" (*RTL* 76). This turns out to be a cultural imperative for the characters in Shepard's plays like one of the characters of Edward Albee's in *Who's Afraid of Virginia Wolf,* who discloses, "one needs an illusion which is a historical imperative". Similarly, the characters, who emerge in Shepard's play with an ambition to represent the values and the resonances of the legendary mythic figures, do not, in fact, exist apart from being a reflection of the grand falsehood on the basis of which they get constructed. Shepard clarifies, 'through bragging a lot of early days American heroes sprang up. Paul Bunyan, Pecos Bill all those mythic guys emerged from fantastic 'tall tales', mostly based on macho bravado and superhuman strength. But these guys are totally fictions (*RTL* 76). Thus all characters' grip on reality is constantly elusive, it doesn't allow him to form his self definition.

This cultural dislocation has not only affected the concept of self identity but has disrupted the basic foundation of linguistic communication. The certainty inherent in a rural establishment is no longer resourceful to language. For Shepard, "language comes from the earth, if a man raised on a mountain, he's going to talk according to that place" (qtd. in Goldberg 44). With the change of the cultural context and economic transformation, language too has evolved into a new entity. The questions Shepard raises are whether an artist can create under such repressive circumstances, or can an artist reproduce an emotional image of his own self through his creations? Can an artist locate the originality of his being ? Reconstruction of cultural myths and its eventual merger with the constructed mythology is what forms one of the basic fundamental aspects of creative struggle in Shepard's plays.

III

The characters, in their bid to rediscover the lost space of mythological cartography, at times, are on the move to reach that eluding locale what they consider as home. As explained by Kosmo, in *The Mad Dog Blues* (1971)[6], they "move (s) from spot to spot across the planet hoping to find a home" because that is where, he believes, lies his 'roots' (*MDB* 155). The characters in Shepard take upon themselves the task to explore the possibilities to form new myths. Mark Siegel calls this a return "to the roots of so many American myths." (235)

Against the blinding thickness of material objects in urban America, the artists make desperate attempts to disengage themselves from their immediate reality.

Shepard notes, "(Americans) temperamentally come from the country, they come from that particular sort of temporary society, that you find in southern California, where nothing is permanent, where everything could be knocked down, and it would not be missed, and (from) the feeling of impermanence that comes from that –that you don't belong to any particular culture" (qtd. in Kenneth Club 198).

Sam Shepard has assumed the image of a Shaman, a magician to exorcise evil elements from American civilisation. Shepard confides: "What I'm trying to get at here," says Shepard, is that real quest of a writer to penetrate into a world. A world behind the form ... .The power of words for me isn't so much in the delineation of a character's social circumstances as it is in the capacity to evoke visions in the eyes of the audience. American Indian poetry ... is a prime example. The roots of the this poetry stem from a religious beliefs in the word itself. Words as living incantation" (qtd. in Siegel 236–237).

Shepard's characters are also found to have been engaged in the exercise of penetrating into "the mythic world beneath the form" which is "reality" for them but as Siegel observed, this "reality" of the world most often is more "violent contradictory" and "ultimately inescapable" (237).

The play *The Mad Dog Blues*, is defined by George Stambolian as an allegory of the American "brain" (83), wherein the characters, who are actively engaged in search of identity and roots, mostly look at the world through the images provided by the media and the myths of American culture. The protagonist, Kosmo, is a popular culture poseur who dresses like the rock 'n' roll star of the '60s (green velvet satin cape with tight pants, tease hair and no shirt, carries a Congo drum – *MDB* 148). He tries to reflect the qualities of a rock star, assigned by the media, through his personality, that of a sado-masoachist, intuitive, without any control over his primeval violence coupled with the characteristic abhorrence of politics, philosophy or religion yet he takes resource to God showing his slim connection with the fundamental cultural reference to faith; he "gropes in the dark without a game". The act reminds him of his spatial existence in vulnerable uncertainty.

This play is about an artist's awareness of 'Americanness'. Stambolian writes, "(It) is clearly an American play, and only an imagination that has grown on American movies, radio shows, pulp magazines and music could have conceived it" (81-82). The play is collage of character from American popular culture. There is Yahoodi, dressed in black and who is "like a big city dope dealer" (148) with an Indian flute; Marelene Dietrich wears short shorts, lots of make up, high heels and carries a whip; Mae West is in an evening gown with a feather boa drops from her famous movies who is tough and sexy. Paul Bunyan is there with his ox and waco and he moves around with his broken guitar like "Sad Gabby Hayes".

Kosmo, the protagonist, makes desperate moves to relocate his home and this voyage for home brings him to the 'contingency' of encountering a vision which too comes to him through the metronomic rhythms of Jimmy Hendrix. Kosmo's voyage is almost a Homeric Odyssey which makes the hero encounter unpredictable events in the undetermined trajectories of his journey. Like Ulsses, too, encounters a series of events. From his home – the space of crude certainty, equilibrium and repression – he is transported by the rhythmic vision of Jimmy Hendrix to the 'urban clusters of tangents', to a "jungle" which is, claims his sidekick Yahoodi, the place where he can "write" (*MBD* 151). And the city, says Kosmo, "getting me down. Too many tangents. It's no place to collaborate." (*MDB* 151). Hence, he moves to rediscover the interior territory of the self which inspires Marlene Dietrich to sing Blues, 'Jungen Mensch' like Janis Joplin:

> They don't yet know who they are
> Silly boys, just young man following a star
> ....
> And loneliness comes like a dart
> There's nothing to find till you find your heart.
> (*MDB* 151–52)

The characters, in their outward venture to get to the reachable memory of their collective consciousness, are involved in the exercise of reconstructing the myths to contextualise their existence with a linear narrative in order to integrate the silent and the discontinued spaces with invented history. The characters of the play are engaged in the act of exploring the promised roots, the finality of which reaches the pinnacle with the ritual of self-destruction; spiritually in *Mad Dog Blues*, and physically in *Tooth of Crime* and *Suicide in B-Flat*.

The extrapolation of the self has different purposes for different characters. Yahoodi has undertaken the expedition to become 'famous' by endorsing the popular image of a famous person. To be famous for Yahoodi is to be able to "fly back to the city and put a needle in (his) arm! ... buy a farm in the country and raise a family and be a happily married man." (*MDB* 154). But for Kosmo, the journey is an artistic compulsion, because he realises, "I'm a musician! I've got to create! I've got to get back to the city. Back to my band. Back to my roots. I've lost touch with my roots" (155). He is anxious because as he says, "If I miss my moment in history, it may never happen again" (154).

But the mythical search for the treasure in the wilderness, which even instigated them to commit the primitive crime of homicide, treachery and even theft, turns out to be a desperate drive just for a sackful of market garbage which mockingly reduced the imagined self dignity of a cowboy hero and turns him in to a garbage gleaner carrying heaps of cold drink bottle caps – a sweeping symbol of the American market capitalism and the culture of mass consumption. They utterly fail to transcend the repressive reach of market capitalism and trespass the parameters of values constituted by the ethics of consumerism. The "tons of bottles caps", which they thought to be heaps of gold, screamed loudly only to remind them of the futility of the attempts to find out the purpose of existence, and these American drifters become aware of the terrible actuality about the irreplaceable silence of their a historic continuity and the subsequent impossibility to construct even an illusion of heroic prehistory. This tragic inability of the artist to construct the illusion even of an invented history displaces him from his quasi-stable locale and turns him into a cultural nomad which disempowers him from the ability to create owing to the obvious absence of any reference, owing to the terrible knowledge about the eternal absence of a home. The song that emanates from the inner core of their emotions turns out to be an elegy on the death of home:

> Cause ya know that I'm true believer
> In
> Home
> ....
> Cause home is any place you feel
> Like
> Home
> ....
> Home is like a rolling stone
> Home is holding something you own
> Your own
> Home
> ....
> My spinning brain is a failure
> With no home
> Ride me in a passenger train
> Move me against the grain
> Move me
> Home.
>
> (*MDB* 194–195)

Shepard's protagonists are icons of a cultural universe where the hegemony of the market discourse predominates. The characters, being embedded entities within that discourse, are forced to assume the identity given by the market. In the system the artist is fatally engaged in a process that eventually ensures the subordination of the artist's subjectivity.

IV

Geography of a Horse Dreamer (1974) deals with this issue of the artist's conflict between his private vision and social exploration. The play, unlike Shepard's earlier plays, has a thematic directness and clarity though the play as a whole is an extended metaphor for the personal dilemma of the artist himself. The play has obvious connections with Shepard's own psychic biography. The play's first performance in 1974 received favourable reviews for its transparency. B.D Young in his review of the play in *Financial Times* (22 Feb. 1974) lauded the play for its comprehensibility so did Irving Wardle in *London Times* who even found the play to have "Old fashioned plot development" (22 Feb, 1974). Shepard brings out his spontaneity as a playwright in this play by an eclectic mix of character types, surprise plot twists and unmotivated behavioural turns.

The play puts a dreamer as the protagonist who is kidnapped by gangsters to force the dreamer to dream the winning number of race horses. But he loses his gift, and cannot dream the winners any more because he has been displaced from the space where lies the roots of his creative power. He eventually goes mad and a doctor tries to perform a surgery on him to remove the 'dream bone' from his nape. At that time his two brothers from Wyoming, his native place, come to rescue him. They kill the gamblers and take away their brother to Wyoming.

The play is defined as "a translation play" by Ross Wetzteon because the audience/spectator has to translate the plot into meaning ("Looking A Gift Horse Dreamer" 133). The play reflects Shepard's own crisis as an artist and his experience of being gradually enfolded by different forces that encroached upon his freedom. Cody, the dreamer in Geography, who is gifted to dream the winning number of race horses is forced to dream the winning number of dogs, a humiliating assignment for the play of Cody. The playwright Shepard is also kidnapped by the cultural entrepreneurs, like Santee and Beaujo, initially through the Obie awards. Cody was also brought to prominence by the publicity in *Life* magazine through which he was noticed by the gangsters who kidnapped him. Shepard was writing plays in the Off Off Broadway production centres where he could easily give his dreams a shape for he had no commercial stakes. But like Cody, Shepard too was almost hijacked by big production houses of Broadway that produced his later plays including *Buried Child* (1996).

As Cody was demoted as dreamer – from a house dreamer to dog dreamer – so was Shepard from a playwright of the *Off Broadway* to a writer for Broadway and finally as a Hollywood screenplay writer (*Zabriskie Point*. 1968 and *Paris, Texas,* 1984). Shepard is torn by the conflict between dreams and power, between talent and its exploitation. Like Cody, Shepard's visionary gifts are also used by the system operations for their commercial gain. Shepard longs to escape to the bucolic world of the "Golden West" of his youth to renew his association with his roots.

Geography of a Horse Dreamer was written when Shepard was in London where he went with the desperation of finding a new purpose in life. The play *Geography* was first produced in England itself (*Theatre Upstairs,* 21 Feb, 1974, directed by Sam Shepard) in which he offered the Royal Court patrons a taste of popular American imagination found in gangster movies, TV western, detective pulp fiction, etc. The play in fact harkens back to a popular American stage comedy of the 1930s *Three Men on a Horse* which also involves racing, gangsters and prognostication. Shepard's *Blue Bitch* (1973)[7] was a precursor to *Geography* which was written for presentation on BBC's "Open House" series.

Cody, the creative visionary who is driven to madness by the psychic accuracy of his dreams, depicts Shepard's concern with an artist's subjugation to the market place which reflects the crisis of the creative of the creative impulse itself. Creativity is the prerogative of a sovereign man which involves "spontaneity and intuition." It is almost an epiphanic experience. In *Geography*, this "rhapsodic mode of creation" is analogous to the phenomenon of dreaming – the sign of Cody's creative gift. Recalling his early process of dreaming, Cody recalls, "It was accidental. It sorta' come to me outa' the blue... At first it was all instinct. Now it's work" (*GHD* 94).

The artist is literally arrested by the gang of Fingers and is locked in a decrepit hotel room that has a pungent stink and jagged wallpaper. Where Cody lies spreadeagle with his legs and hands handcuffed and with the dark sunglasses on even when he sleeps, measures taken to allow Cody uninterrupted dreams where his abductors expect him to come across the winning number in the horse race. His position is described by Santee, one of the side kicks of the gang, as a "crucified position" (88) of "Mr. Artistic Cowboy" (86). Cody is entrapped in almost a Foucauldian Panopticon[8] that prevents him from having any access to the world outside. He is under constant surveillance to ensure that he cannot make any other movement that falls outside the abductor's space. Under the circumstances, to the horror of Santee and Beaujo, the prophetic accuracy of Cody's dream diminishes. Cody is exposed to an alien environment which cannot provide the artist the "connections," where he cannot get what he calls "fresh air." He looks for a situation where his "blood can move again." Here he finds his "dream are jagged. (He) gets a fuzzy picture. Sometimes the numbers blur." (89).

In the claustrophobic incarceration, Cody is absolutely disempowered through the process of a new power relation that successfully subjugates the subject through eventual co-optation into the larger narrative. He does not have any access to power nor to knowledge. Power is operated by his abductors and knowledge is mediated through them in a form that would serve the interest of the forces that control him. The reach of this force is so pervasive that he realises the impossibility to ever escape from there. His body has almost been totally enslaved. He assures Santee, "I've been with it too long Shantee. I couldn't run out or ya' now. I'd be lost. It's been years. I've been blindfolded and shuffled from one hotel to another for as long as I can remember. The sun would probably blind me. Where would I go if I did escape? (88)"

Cody has been perfectly subjected by the forces that aim to reify his creative gifts. He has been reduced almost into a mechanical device programmed to dream the necessary numbers but when he, quite predictably, fails to do so, Santee and Beaujo lament the tremendous fall of their hostage from grace. In fact, by displacing Cody from the realms of knowledge and power his state has been exposed to one of "suspended extinction," for knowledge and power are a hyphenated abstractions or to put in a quantum mechanic jargon, "entangled." They are predicated upon each other which creates the condition for the subject to survive in a society. Power produces knowledge and it is knowledge on the other hand that extends and reinforces power. The artist in Shepard is separated from these two basic sources of empowerment that results in his inevitable doom.

Cody in the play undergoes almost the Foucauldian process of subjugation in which both body and mind are put through a process of arduous and torturous training in order to make the subjected body into a device. The artist, in the process, loses ownership over his own body. When Cody was ordered to take a walk by Santee ("come on take a walk Mr. Artist. It may be your last for a while," 89) while trying to get up from his bed, he struggles to gain muscular control and tries to move his limbs very slowly to figure out how they work. His abductors on the other hand, are desperate to ensure that he remains absolutely ignorant about his own spatio-temporal dislocation a space without geography.

Santee, one of the abductors, suggests, "We might arrange some fresh air. May be. His gotta be blindfolded though. He can't know where he is. That's the chief thing that Fingers impressed upon us. He can't for a second know what is outside the room he's locked up in. Otherwise it spoils the dreaming. He can't know the time either (91)."

The lack of geography prevents Cody from dreaming. The artist fails to regain his visionary gift because of the obvious absence of space. He needs his own 'inner library" – "the inside one," the "space inside" from where the dream comes." He urges, "It's gotta be created. That's what Fingers don't understand. He thinks it's just like it was when I started... He's blocked up my senses. Everything forces itself on the space I need. There's too much chaos now. He'll never get a winner out of me till the space comes back (92)."

The play reflects an artist's quest for substance and solidity. The aesthetic enterprise is intimately linked to locations. Shepard once wrote, "I have a feeling that the cultural environment one is raised in predetermines a rhythmical relationship to the use of words ("Inner Library," 52). That geo-cultural space determine the private universe of an individual in which one thinks, perceives and experiences reality. Shepard has named this stored images of personal predisposition as "inner library." For he, given his own "inner library," admitted to having become none other than an "American writer." Likewise, Cody can dream only "American dream" for this is the American space that his lost, his place of origin. His ability to dream the winning horses in advance is originally tied to his Wyoming native home and its bucolic environs. With a bid to regain his lost ability he urges for the regeneration of his "internal environment" (94). To fulfil this mission he makes mental attempts to reach the locale of his fading memories in order to restore his original identity and his creative self. His desperation for his old space is tellingly underlined:

> Why is he (Fingers) keeping me on ! I wanna go back to Wyoming and raise sheep. That's all I wanna do. I got no more tips. I'm from the great plains, not city. He's poisoned my dreams with these cities. (96)

Cody's separation from his native space makes him intently aware of the necessity of his own space for the purpose of his creative exercise. For him this is the uncontaminated American landscape where his creative roots are nestled. The anarchy of the cityscape arrests the creative self of the artist and eventually pushes the artists into a state of creative bankruptcy. Ironically, the crime syndicate kingpin, Fingers, orders his men – Beaujo and Santee – to ensure that Cody is not at all interfered by the surroundings or other outside objects which Fingers suspected might upset the flow of Cody's dreams. But Fingers fails to understand that Cody's isolation and relocation have destroyed his sense of Geography from where the images of his dreams come. Cody's displacement, therefore, jeopardises the authenticity of the whole process of dreaming. This decentring of Cody is an agonising experience because his dreams have to be produced in a state of void without having any reference. Cody finds it, "Stupid! It's really stupid! I'm dreaming American horses and wee are probably in Morocco somewhere. It don't make sense. I gotta know where we are so I can adjust. I've lost track of everything. I need some landmarks." (94-95)

But Beaujo reminds him of what Fingers had told him "dream are a gift from God. It don't matter what country you dream in." Cody is furious at Fingers's unwarranted interference to stipulate the methodology of accomplishing an act of pure creativity. He retorts: "Fuck Fingers! I'm the dreamer. I ought to know." (95)

Cody is a peculiar product of the American paradox. His roots are in the American landscape. The west is his home. The great plains, the subject of his dream ("I dream about the great plains," 92). The "Cowboy Artist" belongs to the place of "Real Cowboys in leather craps" (116). Even Fingers recalls the native space of Cody from where he was abducted with deep nostalgia: "Oh what a town! Saloons with Winchester rifles tacked up on the wall … . Indians shuffling the dusty streets. Buffalo Bill's name plastered on everything. And at night. At night it was magical. Like praying. I never heard such a silence as that. No where on the earth. So vast and lovely. Just the brisk cold night blowing in through the hotel window. And outside, the blue peaks of the big horn mountains. The moon shinning on their snowy caps. The prairie stretching out and out like a great ocean. I felt that God was with me. The earth held me in its arms." (*GHD* 116)

Fingers's nostalgic recitation of the space of Cody's creative inspiration carries dramatic significance which directs attention to the invocation of the American West which constitutes one of the key elements in the play. Like Cody, Shepard himself has drawn his inspiration from the Western experiences. His sojourn in London, where he wrote the play, provided him the vantage to accentuate his regard for geography and sensibility of place. And Shepard, in casting a glance back across the Atlantic, envisages not only the America of conflagrant contemporary—time but also "the country of a century past" (Wade, 63). His deployment of Western motifs, the reconstruction of its iconography, link the playwright a deep rooted notion of Americannesss which resides in the play with a resonance that echoes long held notions of the national character. It is the American geography, the American aesthetics and the American music, that created Cody. The continued survival of Cody is subjected to the availability of these contexts, else he would be without history – a contextualised. In order to get back his "local frequency", he requires to relive his sources of belongingness. He wants a pure vision of the West and listen to his records again. "If I could just listen to my records again. That's all. Just a couple of tracks off my record... And all of them came from the music. It's a source of inspiration" (99). For Santee, who symbolises deadly commercial entrepreneurship, Cody's quest for his lost space is just a "cocka' shit", who considers the allowance to Cody to have "three squares a day was enough. The movement through the room" (109) was more than enough for anybody "to dream". But it is Beaujo who casts a doubt on their own understanding of Cody's dream. He suspects: "May be his dreaming does take on a kind of an art form, the way he does it. It might need some special stuff to get him back in top form." (90)

Beaujo is also disturbed when Cody's area of activity has been shifted from horse racing to greyhound racing. Beaujo does not approve of the shift which is not only disgraceful to the artist but their own sense of respectability as well. Besides, the cruelty, Cody is subjected to, terrifies Beaujo because Cody is used as a mere object that can dream the numbers which have commercial potentialities. He apprehends, "he can't suddenly change his whole style of dreaming like that, it might kill him" (95) because that is a completely new area of operation for the artist who "don't know a greyhound from a crocodile" (95). But Cody's inability to dream gets into the nerve of Santee because his own fate is closely linked with Cody's success. It's the dream of Cody that would ensure him at least "a little room service and a color TV" (103). Cody is not only the victim of his gifts, Santee too is a victim who is doomed to have his fate determined by someone's abstract, mysterious abilities. Cody's mysterious creative gift was evolved through his American experience of the West and its music. Ironically, it threatens his own freedom because of his being within an American space where media has a determining dominance. The media exposure has dehumanised him for he was considered as a means to earn fortune. Even his brothers, who would eventually rescue him from the gangsters, also started cashing in on Cody. Cody weakly recalls, "I had that big dream... then *Life magazine* ... then folks started cashing in. My brothers" (97).

Cody' fame turned on himself by taking away his freedom. His fame made him "the hottest thing in the West." And the gangsters intervened. He was wined, he was dined and he was kidnapped. He finally interpellates the new compulsions and almost mechanically goes through a process of regeneration that conditions him to dream the greyhounds, suggesting final degeneration of the artist. He dreams the Black Beaujo was the potential winner in the dog race. And immediately the condition of his abductors changes as Beaujo says, "the slump is over" (102). Cody's dream follows a candid confession of Santee that reflects the hopeless web that entraps everybody. Santee's inhuman treatment to Cody is justified by Santee's own existential compulsions:

> May be I was pushing it too hard. This better be it boy or we're all gonna cut up in little pieces and mailed to our Mammas. I know you ain't used to working under pressure but that's how it is. It's like snake bitin' its own tail... For a solid month you was right. You was so right that you had somebody out there eatin' turtle soup and fillet mignon three times a day. Being Chauffer driver to the grocery store. That's how it is you got genius somebody else got the power. (102-103)

Cody's own power makes him powerless, he even fails to retain his equilibrium. He even loses his physical identity as he is possessed by the local dream frequency that makes him speak in foreign accent (he begins to speak in Irish accent), he is transformed into a dog breeder and by the time Fingers arrives with the Doctor, he has been transformed into a dog, whimpering and scurrying away from the other characters, crashing into the things like frightened animal. Santee says "(we) can pet him." (110).

Cody reflects Shepard's own crisis with geographical displacement. His stay in England had its apparent impact on his work that forced him to "Anglicize" his work. He mentions in "Inner Library":

> I noticed … after living in England for three straight years, that certain subtle changes occurred in this rhythmic construction (of language). In order to accommodate these new configurations in the way a sentence would over blow itself (as is the English tendency). I found myself adding English characters to my plays. ("Inner Library" 216).

But the doctor who arrives on the scene with Fingers, displays the horrible ignorance about the whole process of creativity when he tries to interpret the creativity in terms of certain biological properties.

He even proceeds to perform a deadly surgery upon Cody to remove his "neck bone" which he described a source of Cody's magical power and how the power can live on if the bones is transplanted on Beaujo with simple surgical accuracy.

At this point two brothers of Cody storm in to rescue him from the Brits and their effete bejewelled ring leader by having all of them shot down (like an unexpected *deus ex machina*). But the reality of the two brothers remains ambiguous. Jasper and Jason, the six-foot-five-inches tall, huge figures, carrying double barrel guns and knocking the adversaries in a flash, look almost like the images of Cody's final dream, the last metaphor of Cody's creative ability to shape his own life.

The play almost overtly acknowledges that tradition, geography, rootedness and identity need to coalesce, for poetic art owes more to ground than flight of fancy. That is why the inexorable effort to force-feed him Americana and American record albums and nauseam predictably fail to bring back Cody's frequency.

How agonizing the effect of this apparent comedy could be on an artist can well be judged by Bob Dylan's reaction to the last scene of the play during the play's Manhatta Theatre Club production. As the main character in the play was about to be shot by a hypodermic syringe, Dylan stands in the row and yells in the hall, "Wait a minute! Wait a second! Why's he got the shot? He shouldn't get the shot! The other guy should get it! Give it to the other guy!" All his companions, embarrassed at the situation, try to control Dylan by hauling him back down to his seat. Finally, Dylan leaps up again, "I DON'T HAVE TO WATCH THIS! DIDN'T COME HERE TO WATCH THIS!" (qtd. in *RTL* 181)

Shepard addresses the issue of cultural translocation of artist into the realm of reification where the artist is no longer ensconced in the comfort of his native space. An artist is not recognised "just as a man" but as an "industry" which can be controlled and manipulated by the corporate operators. He has captured the cultural context where the equations of power relations have altered. Creative ability and artistic refinement cannot protect an artist as he can easily be arrested and subjugated by the gigantic forces that have reconstructed the social space through their sheer expertise of controlling the systems of cultural operations where mechanical power takes over creative and artistic power.

The artist becomes an easy prisoner within the system that gradually shuts him round in a vacuum. But then Shepard's heroes regenerate new strategies to preempt their disfiguration. Like Cody, they finally overpower the subjugating forces through imaginations and inventions at different dimensions. The artist seems to follow Waco's inspiring instruction in *MDB*: "Just follow your heart. That's what a man is supposed to do. The only thing a man can do. Just follow your heart". (158).

NOTES AND REFERENCES

1. *Feuilleton* is the salon attire (of a literature) which was fundamentally designed to be sold in the streets (See Walter Benjamin, Cales Baudlaire, *A Lyric Poet in the Era of High Capitalism*. London: NLB (1973) 35.
2. *Cowboy Mouth* was first produced at the American Place Theatre on April 29, 1971, as an after piece of *Back Dog Beast Bait*.
3. The book *Tack 'n' Togs*, Dealer Round Up Report No. 2 (Minneapolis 1972) records, as per the survey undertaken, Western vests are sold more in New York, Pennsylvania and New England than in Texas and Oklahama, showing the urban urge to artificially obtain intimacy with myths.
4. Linda Hart defines 'historiographic metafiction' as the blending of brute events of the past and the historical fiction we construct out of them (See John M. Durvell, *Modern Fiction Studies*. 43:3 Fall (1999) 562).
5. Elizabeth Proctor argues that Shepard's equation of myth and mystery has problematised several general areas such as art (what is it?), (Where does it come from? What is an art?), Identity (the quest for roots) and reality (What is?). (See "Off Beat Humour and Comic Mystery in Shepard's Plays" in Kind Kimball. Ed.(1988) 39).
6. *The Mad Dog Blues* first produced by Theatre Genesis at St. Mark's Church in the Bowery on March 4, 1971, directed by Robert Glaudin.
7. *Blue Bitch* is about an American couple –Cody and Dixie. They try to sell their greyhound with the help of a cockney milkman. The milkman gradually metamorphose into a canine like beast and it results in eventual breakdown in communication.
8. Foucault has interpreted the post eighteenth century articulation of power in terms of Jeremy Bentham's Panopticon which according to Foucault accurately captures the structure of power relation in the nineteenth century. Panopticon is a circular building enclosing a central inspection tower. It allows for the invisible surveillance of a large number of inmates by relatively smaller number of people. It reflects the theoretical formulation of nineteenth century penology which emphasizes disciplining of the body through the techniques of real or perceived surveillance. Foucault observes that the unstable history of penal system is associated not only with the perception of the criminals, but also on the changes engendered by the emergence of institutions dealing with the formation of knowledge. Thus is knowledge linked to power and the prison becomes a tool of knowledge. The emergence of disciplinary institutions in society give rise to prison. Panopticon perfectly fulfils the requirement of constant observation. (See Michael Foucault *Discipline and Punish*: *The Birth of the Prison* (1975). Trans. Alan Sheridan. London: Allen Lane, 1977.)

Works Cited

Bauman, Zygmunt. *Postmodernity and Its Discontents*. (1997).

Chubb, Kenneth. Interview. "Metaphor, Mad Dog Blues and Old Time Cowboys." *American Dream*. Ed. Bonnie Maranca, (1981).

Coe, Robert. "Image Ghosts are Blown." *The Rock Plays*. Bonnie Maranca. Ed. (1981).

Foucault, Michel. "Nietzche, Geneology, History". *Language, Counter Memory, Practice: Selected Essays and Interview*. Eds & trs. D.F. Bounchard and S. Simon. Oxford: Blackwell, 1977.

Goldberg, Robert. "Sam Shepard: Off Broadway's Street Cowboy." *Rolling Stone College Paper* Oct. 1980.

Goldman, Lucien. "The Genetic Structuralist Method in the History of Literature." *Towards a Sociology of the Novel*. Tr. Alan Sheridan. London: Tavistock, 1975.

Protor, Elizabeth. "Off Beat Humours & Comic Mystery in Shepard's Plays." *La Turista*, The Unseen Hand, "*The Dog Blues and The Forensic and the Navigators*." Sam Shepard: A Case Book. Ed. King Kimball. NY: Garland Publishing Inc., 1988.

Rosen, Carol. "*Emotional Territory: An Interview with Sam Shepard*." MD 30: (1993).

Savage Jr., William W. "*The Cowboy Myth*," The Cowboy: Six Shooters, Songs & Sex. Eds. Charles W. Harris & Buck Raimy. Oklahama: University Press, 1975.

Selden, Ramon. *The Theory of Criticism*. London: Longman, 1988.

Shepard, Sam. *Rolling Thunder Logbook*. New York: Limelight Edn., 1987.

_____*Cowboy Mouth. Food For Love and Other Plays* (1984).

_____*The Mad Dog Blues and Other Plays* (1972).

_____*Melodrama Play, Angel City and Other Plays* (1977). Maranca (1981).

_____*Geography of a Horse Dreamer*. London: Faber and Faber, 1977.

Sheridan, Alan, *Michel Foucault: The Will to Truth*. New York: Travistock Publications, 1982.

Siegel, Mark. "Holy Ghosts: The Mythic Cowboys in the Plays of Sam Shepard". *Rocky Mountain Review* 36: 4 (1982) 238-39.

Stambolian, George. *A Trip Through Popular Culture: Mad Dog Blues*. Bonnie Maranca, Ed. (1981)

Wade, Leslie, A. *Sam Shepard and the American Theatre*. Wertwood : Greenwood press, (1997).

Wadle, Irving. Review. (Theater Upstairs Production). "Geography of a Horse Dreamer." *London Times* Feb. 22, 1974.

Wetzsteon, Ross. "Looking a Gift Horse Dreamer in the Month." *American Dream*. Ed. Bonnie Maranca. New York: Performing Arts Journal Publications, 1981.

Wetzsteon, Ross. Introduction. *Fool for Love and Other Plays of Sam Shepard*. New York: Bantam Books, 1988.

Williams, Raymond. *The Long Revolution*. Harmondsworth: Penguin, 1965.

Young, B.A Review. "Theatre Upstairs: *Geography of a Horse Dreamer*." *Financial Times,* Feb. 22, 1974.

5

Assertions against Appropriation: Rock and Jazz Stars and Counter culture Heroism

Shepard has created his protagonists from his own artistic experiences. He is an intimate insider to the American cultural landscape. He has been a part of the world that his dramatic characters encounter. For him, therefore, the experience of the artist-protagonist is more an extended metaphor of his own subjective experiences than a depiction of a fictionalised world. He has diverse commitments to different art forms-music is one of them.

Music has assumed a significant position in Shepard's emerging pattern of plays which not only provides a vantage to look at the conditions of the artists' world, it has also evolved itself into a means for redefining the changing realities that the artist is almost inescapably linked with. Here in this chapter, two of the most significant plays of Sam Shepard are taken up where music assumes the role of a character – *Tooth of Crime* (1972)[1] and *Suicide in B-flat* (1976)[2]. The first one portrays a rock icon Hoss as its protagonist when the second one features Niles, a Jazz maestro as the central figure of the play.

Sam Shepard has been a part of the world of rock music. As a musician he was quite close to Bob Dylan. His intimacy became closer with Dylan through his taking part in the Rock Odyssey, Rolling Thunder Revue, as a writer, and he travelled with Dylan and his group across America as a part of the team. He, however, gained a distance from the Rock music world of

America when he moved to London where he had written two very significant plays with American artists as protagonists: *Tooth of Crime* (1972) and *Geography of Horse Dreamer* (1974).

Rock in America is different from pop and rock 'n' roll music owing to its different ideological orientation. Rock music has, as Peter Wicke has pointed out, "a political ambition" (*Rock Music* 1990). Simon Frith observes that the organising logic of rock has not been the intention of making money by fulfilling certain market criteria but to express commitment to music itself (qtd. In Wicke 161). Rock music, in fact, evolved through the artist's artistic and political perceptions. Shepard, in fact, was very much influenced by Bob Dylan who had given rock music a strong political dimension. Dylan's "The Answer my friend, is/ Blowin' in the wind" soon became a battle hymn against racial segregation in America. Dylan even led, with Martin Luther King, a column of 20,000 people in the "Great March to Washington" in 1968 to protest against racism. Shepard's romanticism with rock was intensified when he saw rock music evolved into an assertion of social commitment.

Rock was viewed as a clever subterfuge of capitalist interest by the leftists and, on the other hand, the conservatives viewed rock as an anti-American activity because of its obvious rejection of established norms (Wicke 102). However, rock music emerged as a powerful discourse of challenging the established system. Hoss, the hero of *Tooth of Crime,* defines rock as a means to "Go against the Codes". He says, "That's what they used to do. The big one Dylan, Jagger, Townsend. All them cats broke codes. Time can't change that" (*TOC* 209).

As rock succeeded to address social issues radically, the corporate operators arrived in the scenario to convert this music into a commodity. Commercial manipulations took rock music to paradoxical circumstances. This seemingly anti-capitalist art of America has been simulated for mass consumption through the system that the rock had been antagonising. Thus a so-called revolution became a potential object to be promoted as a market commodity. From a maverick, the artist is reduced to a stereotype whose radicalism is also "programmed". In *Tooth of Crime*, Crow, the new generation rock renegade, belongs to such a category. He is an image chaser who is under the compulsion of believing his mask to be his real identity: "But I believe in my mask – the man made up in me. And I believe in my dance – and destiny." (*TOC* 234)

The true artist under such conditions is forced to encounter one of the typical crises of determining the preferences between the two dialectically opposing modes – qualifying the artistic creations with political commitments and quantification of the artistic success in terms of economic pragmatism. The artist finds himself amidst the complex interrelationship between market and ideology. Shepard addresses this crisis of artistic priorities and the paradoxical ideological conflicts in a definite set of plays that can be categorised as his 'Rock Plays'.

In the play the *Tooth of Crime*, we find the old rock singer, Hoss, having failed to resolve this ideological crisis, takes up the drastic step of freeing himself from the repressive and threatening reality by blowing himself up with a gun. This happens in case of Niles as well in *Suicide*. Ironically when 'rock' is assigned to emancipate the individuals trapped in the system after being robbed off their lives, as mentioned by Rogers Waters of the *Pink Floyd*, the musician himself fails to find out means to liberate himself from the trap placed by the system.

The *Tooth* is a play redolent with the historical simulacra of rock music of the late fifties and the sixties as well as the other anti-social paraphernalia like that of gangsterism, gun slinging, and such other elements. The play has the story that is set against the backdrop of rock music taken from a historical perspective to highlight the modernist evolution of rock into a political narrative having its musical base on rhythm and blues that found the pinnacle of its mass success with that unpretensious musical novice, who soon turned into a rock legend, called Elvis Presley. Like Elvis, Hoss in *Tooth* too was an energetic young man, a radical 'fast gun' who also picked up folk music like Dylan. What Hoss wanted to become was "A Man" (277). R & B music, like Presley, was the source of his music and eventually, he got stuck in his invented image. Like Henry Heckamore in *Seduced*, Hoss has his personality dissolved to turn into a "fucking industry" (*TOC* 227) and he eventually degenerates from being an artist to a "chart killer," from being a creator to a "chart climber." Thus begins the Faustian journey of the artist into the dark interior from where the only escape is through self-destruction.

Hoss in the play expresses his awareness of the receding of a centre that provided the space of temporal location to the artist. The locational certainty enabled the artist to evolve the idioms of romantic radicalism. But Hoss laments the passing of the era which Leonard Wilcox defines as the "modernist ethos of artistic mastery and a sense of history and tradition" (61-62). Hoss consciously witnesses his progressive degeneration from being an artist that creates and inspires, to a commodity at the mercy of the market. He is being alienated from his own self and identity. He chronicles this degeneration:

> Backed to a fucking box. I can't believe it. Things have changed that much. They don't even apprentice no more. Just mark for the big one. No respect, no more. When I was that age I would sell my leather to get a creak at a good teacher. I would. And I'd some a' the best,. There is no sense of tradition in the game no more. There's no game. It's just back to how it was. Rolling night clubs. Strip joints. Bustin' up poker games. Zip guns in the junk yard. Rock fights, dirt clods, bustin' windows. Vandals, funkies, West side story. Can't they say where they're goin'! Without a code it's just crime. No art involved No technique, finesse. No sense of mastery. The touch is gone. (*TOC* 219)

The rock singer finds himself stuck in a tricky historical juncture for the rock has been a symphony of protest against the repression of the past meaning and codes of patriarchs. Hoss discovers that the age and ethos have changed.

Jeanette P. Malkin finds the *Tooth of Crime* to be the best play of Shepard. She describes the play as "sci-fi futuristic and on the far side of American Dream." She writes, the play is "Part western, part rock and roll fantasy, it is wholly American in its concerns with frontier roots, success ethics, identity and the hard rock images of a narcissistic pop industry turned into cultural myth" (198).

Shepard addresses the issue of the instability of success and its corrupting effects in a definite set of plays where the

Tooth of Crime occupies a prominent place. The play also takes up one of the most pertinent cultural questions in the capitalist context – what Vivien Patraka has defined as "the archetypal challenge to and replacement of one ageing generation by a younger one" (26). The playwright here reinforces the regenerative power of violence. Violence is accentuated by the apparent division of the two worlds diversely represented by the figures poised against each other in their combat to assert supremacy of the competing ideologies represented by Hoss and Crow respectively. In this conflict, however, Lanier W. Gregory finds certain symmetric equivalences in the structural order of the play (50). There is a balanced division between the two major figures who eventually get actively involved in the clash of two cultural vernaculars of two generations. Despite the apparent separation of the protagonists from each other. Hoss and Crow happen to belong to the same world of rock music with opposing ethos in both physical and ideological terms. When Hoss is in black rocker gear with silver studs and black kid gloves he looks like a mean and slightly young Rip Torn (*TOC* 205). Crow, on the other hand, is like Keith Richard in "high heeled green rock and roll boots, tight greasy blue jeans, a tight yellow T-shirt, green velvet coat (...) and a black eye patch covering the left eye. He holds a short piece of silver chain in his hands and twirls it constantly, tossing it from hand to hand ...." (*TOC* 220).

Hoss represents the ethos prevalent in the rock world of the '60s which was featured by the blue pulse of *Velvet Underground*, Bob Dylan, Crosby Stills and Nash, *Fresh Creams* and others. Crow, on the other hand, represents as described by Lanier, "the flashier edges of the late '60s cool rocker, the throbbing back beat, ironic lyrics, and often complex orchestrations of the *Rolling Stones. The Who, The Doors, Iron Butterfly*. They belong to the world of *Masserati* and *Impala* respectively".

The play focuses on the conflict of the bipolarised ethics of the two contesting generations and subsequent redrawing of the centres of the media centric world. Hoss, the elderly musician, becomes increasingly uncertain about the acceptability of his kind of music – rhythms and blues – which he disturbingly associates with the vanishing of the comforting myth of 'blue suede shoes'. He is frightened to recognise the approaching end of his reign as a rock star which also makes him aware of the fact of his physical ageing and degeneration. His stage appearance too is emblematic of walking on down the hall towards a confrontation with death. The self-deceptive particularity of the inner essence of the personality of Hoss is revealed in his opening song wherein Bruce Powe finds the dream structure against which the play is set (51). That is, the song is the reinforcement of the underlying structure of the theme of the play itself.

> So here's another illusion to add to your confusion
> Of the way things are
> ... .
> So here's another fantasy
> About the way things seem to be to me. (*TOC* 205)

The song is reflective of the world Hoss lives in. This is a world 'adept with illusion' (Powe 51), a world which is illusive and confusing. Hoss's is a world of receding rebellion.

Crow's on the other hand, is a world much younger in taste and temperament. When Hoss's is an "illusion of seeming", Crow's is a world of "conscious deception" (Lanier 52). The determining pattern of Crow's world constituted the leitmotifs that are encored in his song:

> I've fooled the Devil's land
> I've fooled the Ace of spades
> I've called the bluff in God's own face
> Now keep me from my fate. (*TOC* 253)

The tragedy, lies not in mere destruction of the semantic certainty of culture that Hoss represents, it also lies in the conscious awareness of Crow about the improvised self-delusion to invent a fictive reality of his own. Crow, in his bid to save Hoss from being obliterated, instructs him to impersonate Rod Stewart and other starts of rock music to ascertain at least a temporary phase of acceptability. But Hoss rejects the approach. He rejects the process what Ernesto Laclau would call 'homogenisation' and 'essentialisation'.[1] Though Hoss himself has been a precursor of anarchy – 'a killer', a metaphorical expression for entropy, - he refuses to be radically stereotyped and patterned on the basis what Crow seems to have accepted as a *sine qua non* for survival. Even the anti-hegemonising mission of the rock artist ironically turns into a hegemonic cultural discourse within the sub-cultural world of rock. Rock gets manipulated to serve the interests of market ambitions. In the process, the well evolved self-perception of the artist, what he thought to be the valid means of self-understanding, tends to be threatened and jeopardised by the powerful subversions affected by the capitalist by-products like the consciously deceptive artist Crow. When Hoss has an awareness of mythical heroism and his obligation to represent this as a quintessential American cultural identity, Crow appears as a being, oblivious of his own prehistory. Hoss is perpetually reminded of his belongingness to a mythical landscape of possibility by Becky: "But you're a hero now. A hero. All those losers out there braking at the moon." (*TOC* 32)

Becky also defines the underlying philosophy of Hoss's existence – 'power', which is one of the most desired abstract authorities that American heroism is so intimately attached to. This is also considered an end in itself. Becky underlines it: "Power ... that's what you live and die for. Every breath you take you Breathe the power. You live the power. You are the power."(*TOC* 32)

But Crow, on the other hand, proceeds to appropriate the identity of Hoss as his own and is eventually able to walk perfectly like Hoss who is to be sacrificed by Crow ("Crow is into Hoss's walk now and does it perfect", 50). Thus Crow assimilates the identities within himself through an absorption of Hoss's essential rhythmic structures. Gregory Lanier suggests that "Crow becomes Hoss by assimilating the heritage that forms Hoss's musical identity" (55). This act of Crow affects the ritualistic destruction of the original possessor of a tradition, namely Hoss, who is threatened to lose both his musical and physical territory.

The artist's struggle to retain his identity forces him to involve himself with an ontopological search. The Derridean portmanteau word that signifies the rootedness of Being in a spatial location. Hoss, in his attempt to reconstruct his self-identity, recourses to the chronotope of his private history. He finds incidental similarity in his history with that of Crow who recounts his lost, lonely, adolescent days, and who runs, being a runt, "outside the pack" quite like Hoss. But Hoss, despite his incidental commonality of experiences, refuses the complacency of sharing common history by disclosing a brute actuality, "We're punk champs cowerin' under the keepers and the Refs and the critics and the public eye. We ain't free no more. Go dammit! We ain't flyin' in the eye of contempt. We've become respectable and safe. Soft, mushy chewable ass lickers." (*TOC* 217)

He, however, mournfully recollects, "we were warrior once".

The capturing of contesting identities becomes the sole reason for the fierce progression of the lethal rock combat. In the first round of combat Crow's allusions to the past have been rejected by Hoss fearing the blurring of his identity in the emerging hegemony of the familiar reality reconstructed through recollection. The next round of combat finds the reversal of roles to the extent that Hoss here becomes the recollector of history when Crow rejects it for fear of being shorn off anything which he could claim to be his own. Hoss reminds him of the pain of black slave who found solace in letting his anguish out through his music – "Little brother Montegomery with the keyboard on his back" or the 'Hookers movin' toward ivory tinkle", "Diplomats and sailors laid side by side to the blues" (241). Hoss reveals the essential norms of a rocker. "'So ya' wanna be a rocker, Study the moves. Jeny Lee Lewis. Buy same blue suede shoes … . Listen to Jimmy Hendrix, Sound like a Dylan, sound like a jagger, sound like an earthquake all over the fender." (*TOC* 243)

Hoss as an artist denies the shift from 'within to without'. The interiority, i.e., the within, of Hoss is conflicting, scattered, fragmented what Bakhtin suggested in a different context to be folkloric and vernacular that provides an alternative to the outer landscape constructed by the elements taken from without. The world constructed by the elements of the external logic is unifying. Seemingly integrated, hegemonically homogenised so that culture remains within the confines of 'controllable cartographic panopticon'. Hoss, defies the defusion of his personality within the rationalising landscape of the official cultural geography. In doing so he ensures his subsequent self-destruction because he was engaged in the act of carving out a personal space against the wilderness of hegemonic cultural totalitarianism.

The history of rock has never been personal. It always has a composite as well as a collective identity for its fusion and composition of diverse, seemingly disparaging, conflicting sounds, styles, images that eventually achieve unity out of sheer absorption. The rock masterpieces like Lewis's 'Great Balls Fire'; Stewart's "Maggie Mae"; Hendrix's "Are you Experienced"; Dylan's "Sub-terranean Homesick Blues" or Jaggers "Jumping Jack Flash", collectively establish the identity of rock as a communal musical form. Hoss, in his desperate bid to locate the space of privacy, encounters the crude final vision which reflected his desired image not in himself but in Crow – the deliberate impersonator of Hoss. Hoss realises his own presence as an embodiment in absolute absentia. He cries out at Crow: "It's me. He is just like me, only younger. More dangerous. Takes Bigger chances. No doubt. No fear .... Yeah it's me just like I wanted To be." (*TOC* 71).

But Hoss makes laudable attempts to retrieve his heroism. Firstly, by enabling himself to interpret his own destiny by reading his own palm "In the palm of my hand I got the last say" (*TOC* 73). He admits his opponent's strong points: "You are a master adapter. A visionary adapter" (*TOC* 251). But he achieves, in spite of his apparent defeat, an elegant heroism. Hoss declares: "All this collection of torture. It's all yours. You're the winner and I'm The loser. That's the way it stands. But I'm losin' big Crow." (*TOC* 251).

And Hoss does it with the ritual of a final shot into his own mouth. Crow, on the other hand, is doomed to survive with conscious self-deception. Hence his desperate persuasion to convince himself of his own presence: "But I believe in my mask – the men I made up in me. And I believe in my dance – and my destiny." (*TOC* 234).

He, however, is apprehensive, genuinely, of the possible collapse of his entire being and total annihilation, hence he attempts to hide his image from himself allowing the fragile front of masks to keep on rolling over his face so that he remains unreachable even to himself:

> Keep me rollin' down
> Keep me rollin' down
> Keep me in my state a grace
> Just keep me rollin' down (*TOC* 252)

Sam Shepard is a man of multiple talents: a musician, an actor, a writer. All three have informed one another. Shepard uses music in his plays as – "another way of making the invisible present" (C.W.E. Bigsby, 164). Shepard seldom fails to set challenges to the actors and audience alike to break through the carapace of naturalism. There is, what the critics like Bigsby call, a kind of "visceral power to Shepard's work, the sense of the unexpected" (154). A premonition of imminent violence haunts the characters who are menaced by this cognitive ambivalence of violence from within. Bigsby describes Shepard's characters as 'borderline psychotics' who occasionally cross borders and eventually befog and eclipse the boundary lines. Having done this, they 'gestate uncertainty' which threatens the well cultivated orderly edifices and structures of society which then turns such individuals into strangers to pre-empt their further entry into, what Bauman identifies as, "the cognitive, moral, or aesthetic map" of the given social territory.

Shepard makes such a 'social misfit' as the protagonist of his 1976 play, *Suicide in B-flat*. Niles, the protagonist, is a prince of jazz who finally becomes a prisoner of the self as an artist, and to rescue himself from the prison he, as Michael Feingold writes, 'flirts with death'. Feingold in his review of the play in *The Village Voice* (Nov.15, 1976) observes, "Shepard rediscovers life as a mystery out of a torrid flirtation with death" (113). The play was first produced in Yale Reportory Theatre, New Haven, in 1976, directed by Walt Jones. Paul Schierhorn played as Niles, Joe Grafasi played Louis, Cliford David as Pablo, William Hickey and Alina Cuervo played Petrone and Laurcen respectively. This is the play that brought

Shepard to a prominent theatre, "YRT", founded by the Dean of the School of Dramas, Robert Brustein.

Niles, the master of jazz musician enacts his own death to the bafflement of Pablo and Louis, the two detectives, who find it too hard to get a clue as to how and why such a death occurred. Like these two detectives most of the reviews that immediately followed the Yale Repertory Theatre production (1976) of the play found the play 'mysterious' and 'elusive'. "The play was ambiguous and vague like looking at a silhouette through a frosted glass... the play could be enjoyed as a mystery of a mystery, and may be wasn't even worth trying to dissect and analyse. I still have the question in mind" wrote Joseph Pronechen in his review published in the *Trumbull Times* (19).

He, however, reconciled with his position by stating that, *Sucide in B flat* is mysterious, but then, everything in theatre doesn't have to be perfectly clear. If that is the case, then audiences would be sentenced to sitting through replay upon replay of *Barefoot in the Park* or worse yet, *Abre Irish Rose*. He even called Shepard a kind of playwright's version of Salvador Dali's artistic surrealism. He wrote: " As we can be fascinated by Dali's dreams on canvas without trying to interpret them or actually be expected to make out Dali's meaning in then, so, too, we can be engaged by Mr. Shepard's mysterious impressions without herniating our own brains. And neither should we be expected to since Shepard's view of theatre is, in a way, selfishly personal" (19).

Ponechen found its justification for being mysterious in the subtitle of the play: "A Mysterious Overture". As by nature and definition 'mysterious' applies to what excites wonder, curiosity or surprise while baffling an eluding efforts to explain or understand.

Michael Feingold wrote about the play as: "On at least one major count, the fault is Shepard's. He never makes it clear .... Possibly he intends something else, but I can't imagine what: there's no chance of ambiguity on such a point, and beg him to clarify it immediately" (113).

Despite the obvert ambiguity and puzzlement the play generated, *Suicide in B-flat* is part of a dramatic pattern which is typically Shepardian, for it deals with a theme that constitutes one of the major creative obsessions of Sshepard's plays where the artist is in danger of becoming the captive of his own legend. As in *Angel City*, *Seduced, Geography*, *Tooth of Crime*, Shepard here problematises the issue of, "The identity and the ontology of the artist" (Wade, 80) who is living in the backdrop of an 'ambient fear', the term coined by Marcus Doel and David Clark, (qtd. in Bauman (22)). The fear emanates from the perpetual demand upon the artist to over-reach their own limits. It exposes the rift between the artist and the milieu in which he was produced.

The play begins with the intriguing event of the presumable death of Niles under mysterious circumstances. Two detectives, Pablo and Louis, arrive to investigate the incident and unravel the mystery for themselves and the audience as well. Their role is reminiscent of the two grave diggers who attempted to resolve the mystery of Ophelia's death in *Hamlet*. Pablo and Luis got engaged in an exercise of pseudo argument like that of the two grave diggers to explain the riddle of the death of Niles which posed a challenge because the face of the victim was blown off beyond recognition. Pablo and Louis belonged to the world that lies outside the psychic space of an artist. In order to demystify the mystery of the death they were investigating, they tried to reconstruct the event and even the biography of Niles in a rather contrived way. What they tried to do was "Trying to reconstruct the imagination of it" (*SB-b*, 194). This is what forms the first line of the play. Ron Mottram found special dramatic significance of this opening line which, according to him, at the immediate level, refers to the attempt by Pablo and Louis to reconstruct the crime, but the peculiar wording of the statement implies much more. The line, in fact, does not say that they are trying to reconstruct the crime, but, instead, the imagination of it. As they were not witnesses to the crime, wrote Mottram, they could not reconstruct and restage the crime, they could only stage their imaginative concept of a crime. Similarly, the staging of the play is a reconstruction of the imagination of the playwright himself. Ron Mottram defined Pablo and Louis not as mere detectives but as two characters in search of an author like that of Laureen and Petrone, the other two characters of the play, the two young musicians, who were waiting for Niles as they were looking for a musician.

Niles:	What's happened to all of you
Laureen:	We've been waiting
Niles:	For me?
Laureen:	We've been waiting to play (*SB-f* 228).

Niles is apparently reluctant to take the responsibility that his role as an artist entails. He, therefore, tries to escape from the part that was thrust upon him.

"Jazz is freedom," said Duke Ellington, an eminent jazz musician (68). Niles, being a jazz musician was in search of his own freedom what he considered to be his artistic privilege. As a jazz musician freedom is supposed to be an intimate essence of his artistic self. Freedom of Niles is endangered. Niles as an artist is threatened. Hence to pre-empt his absolute obliteration, Niles makes an attempt to disappear, escape from the enclosure in which he was confined. The subtle act of disappearance baffles the individuals like Pablo and Louis who belong to conventional institutions. The play, as rightly identified by Ross Wetzsteon, has a structure that resembles "jazzlike riffs", and the play enters the events through a series of 'confused identity', "invented self, contested dichotomy between 'creativity and power' and the sterility of inherited forms" (13).

Niles was born as an artist and he was born outside the America that he eventually finds himself in. He was born in an "island", in the bucolic frill of the nation. He assumed intimacy with the sound of right at his prenatal state when he heard sound "gurling, pounding under water" and "an ocean of blood swimming around him. Through his veins. Through his mother" (*SB-f* 196). And one day he broke into the light of day and was shocked to discover that "he has voice" (*SB-f* 196). It is the discovery and the experience of his own sound that had made him aware of the presence of his own body. The presence of his physicality could become a private experience only through the intimate noises produced in his body, and "his discovery of 'music' was an experience mediated through his bodily presence—(crack of [his] flesh, [his] heart, squeaking, growing of [his] bones, stretching organs expanding" *SB-f* 197). It was music that made a tangible impact on his body. "It stabs at him. Enters into him and becomes part of his physiology. His physignomy. His psychology. His paraphernalia" (*SB-f* 197), said Louis of Niles.

Body was a significant part of Niles's consciousness. His physical size had an important role to play in the growth of Niles as an artist. "Niles was a big man", said Petrone, "a huge man ... His hands were so huge they could stretch two octaves in a single stroke" (*SB-f* 208). Music is not a mere aesthetic mystery for Niles, it is, rather, an experience that is physically tangible. Therefore, the body becomes a major image in the play. The body provides a fulfilment the world could not provide. Bigsby writes about body to be warm; animate; three dimensional that inscribes its own meaning and generates its own discourse which is "independent of and at a tangent to a verbal language which threatens to pull the self into history. It was its own act of resistance in a world in which the mechanical dominated" (5). It is the body that both confines and sets free the soul of the artist. Niles, therefore, gets engaged in an exercise of destroying the "bodies" to recreate new ones to get hold of that elusive freedom. Niles was caught in an ambivalent environment surrounded by music. Music, his most prized sudden discovery, "disappointed" as well as "exhilarated" him. It disappointed because it was "organised", structured, ("Music as an extension of sound. An organisation. Another way of putting it. He's disappointed" *SB-f* 197). But he was at the same time exhilarated "because he sees an opening, an Adventure" (*SB-f* 197). As a jazz musician he had, what Marsalis would call, "structured freedom", "freedom with restraint" (80). Niles made attempts to break through the barriers following the wakes of his radical "revelations", "putting any two things together (that) produces sound ...

striking, plucking, blowing, rubbing, dropping, kicking, kissing ..." (*SB-f* 197). It is the act of subversion of the conventional form that terrified the establishment which was threatened of being derationalised and disrupted. He had put it to such an extent that, pointed out Louis, "most men considers [it] dangerous and suicidal" (*SB-f* 197). His musical productions were abundant and nonstop which was "Endlessly winding through unheard-of-before symphonies. Concertos beyond belief" (*SB-f* 197), Jazz is a musical form, which, unlike pop, is an "infinite challenge" (Marsalis 67). Niles had mastered this art form vis-à-vis the act of posing challenges. He not only placed his music, but his life, as well as his death, at a level located beyond the cognitive reach of the commoners. His music and life were composed in a fashion that follows the typical pattern of jazz syncopation where rhythm falls apart. The syncopation in jazz is an approach that forces the rhythm to do the unexpected by challenging its patterns. As Marsalis talks of Jazz, he says, it challenges the form and parameters by improvising the rhythms and harmonies, and messing up with the boundaries. This music provides Niles the ritual to reach out to "A new dimension" (*SB-f* 220), Hence Pablo and Louis remain absolutely clueless about its perspective.

Even the music of Petrone, one of the apprentices of Niles, is also a kind of "unheard-of-music" in its literal sense of the term. Louis and Pablo could only see the act of playing the saxophone by Petrone, but could not hear any sound coming out of the instrument. The music apparently cannot be comprehended by the detectives in both sensuous and intellectual terms. Petrone explained the reason to them: "Well it takes a while to attune your ears to the frequency we're playing in. It's extremely high. Dogs can't even hear it. That's why Niles has trouble selling it. (*SB-f* 204).

Niles, as well as his co-artists, failed to communicate sand exchange dialogues with his supposed audience. He was an avant-grade artist who was perpetually ahead of the given temporal space. His forward mobility engendered fear in other hence they tried to restrain his movement by forcing some culturally familiar and comfortable identities upon him which initially he voluntarily agreed to accept. He was never a part of the American landscape. He was separated from this territory right from his birth ("I was born in an island. I was not born in America, you know. I was born away, far away, I was imported" *SB-f* 211). His awareness of being an outsider to the given cultural map empowered him to reject the mechanically constructed self of his own being. He asserted the difference through his music. Music became a medium to construct a new set of codes as a counterpoint against the forces of cultural repression and disorientation.

Shepard here has espoused a new position for the artist – 'the fourth dimension'. The dimension at which Niles operates is absolutely different from that of the "two *tough egg* detectives": who even could not notice the physical appearance of Niles on stage because he and Paulette were invisible to others as they used to inhabit in an alternative dimension (83). With the power of the fourth dimension Niles and Paulette planned to remove the encumbrances that affect his creativity. Niles wanted to liberate himself from the conditions that forced him to carry the burden of his own legend. Despite being in the fourth dimension, as Feingold wrote, "Niles is stricken with remorse" (113) mainly because his ritual of murders were mostly the murder of one of his own images. To put it in Feiggold's term, Niles's was the killing not of a victim, but the victim's image of himself (113). Niles faced the daunting task of killing the images of the hero vis-à-vis of himself which he found almost impossible. He became a simulucra and went beyond his control. Like Henry Heckamore (*Seduced*) his own image outgrew his actual identity. He became too big an entity so that he himself became alien to his own image. He was so big that even: "Chicago wouldn't even exist if it wasn't for him. He drove cattle right to Chicago's front door. Town sprang up wherever he stopped to wet his whistle. Crime flourished all around him. The law was a joke to him... He sang songs to the Milky way." (*SB-f* 217).

That was the reason he could not get rid of this identity of his self. "I can't kill a hero! He's a hero", Niles admitted, because one "can't kill a myth" (218). As he changed costumes he adorned the identity of a cowboy like that of Hoss in *Geography of a Horse Dreamer*. He became Pecos Bill, one of the quintessential cowboy images of popular American imagination. This act of adopting identities instigated him to celebrate his supposed immortality. He would sing:

> Pecos Bill, Pecos Bill
> Never died
> And he never will
> Oh, Pecos Bill. (*SBF* 214)

In the process Niles became a redundant entity, a spent force. He has been possessed by the simulated images through subtle persuasion that eventually erased his presence. Paulette reminded him that he had to begin from 'scratch' in order to regain his lost presence, for "now you (Niles) can't get to anything new. It's always the same. You're repeating yourself" (*SB-f* 216). Niles admitted that he was besieged by Voices coming in from all directions that drowned his own. "I'm repeating myself again and again", said Niles. "It's not even myself. I'm repeating them. Over and over. They talk to me all the time. There's Voice Coming At Me" (*SB-f* 216). He became part of a system which Baudrillard would call the "era of the code" wherein the difference between original and copy becomes redundant. It entails reproduction of an object the origin of which is inaccessible and simulation has reached a point of unprecedented importance. Simulation does not only involve the reproduction of a given object it also included the reproduction of labour power of the worker, as in the work of Andy Warhol who went to the extreme to efface the "original" from his artistic practice. He developed a technique to reproduce any number of copies making the original absolutely impossible to be pointed out. This marks the onset of a new era characterised by the erasure of difference between the real and its representation; the original and its copy. The corpse lying in Niles's apartment could not provide any clue to the detectives because they could not ascertain the difference between Niles and the imposter. The couple was faceless but his fingerprints resembled Niles's. Just as the detectives failed to recognise the body, so did Niles failed to recognise himself.

"How could you recognise me when I don't even recognise myself?" Niles asked Petrone.

With a bid to "start from a scratch", Niles recalled his childhood memories to reshape his present reality. His nostalgia for the uncontaminated bucolic past took him to the days when it rained on the corrugated roof of their house that sounded like Belinese cymbals (*SB-f* 211). He would go out with his mother to watch a movie in an army jeep that would run past the rain that was pouring down in a sheet of green jungle water (211). He invented new musical idioms which were apolitical as Laureen commented, "This music has no room for politics." It answered nobody. ."It plays by itself.... It has no boss. Even when the boss is dead it keeps playing" (*SBF* 207). That music suddenly revoked its social context and emerged as an autonomous institution without having any obvious commitment for social communication. Niles could no longer avoid responsibility like that of Shepard. But to remain responsible to a society and a system one must recognise them as respectable institutions. Niles separates himself from any such set-up. His act of killing an unidentified individual is itself an act of rejecting the normative codes of society.

This exactly is the reason that disturbed the self-complacent passivity of Pablo. He laments Niles's act of creatings profane music:

> How does it relate to breaking with tradition! To breaking of with the past. To throwing the diligent efforts of our forefathers and their forefathers before them to the winds! To turning the classics to garbage before our very eyes! To distorting the very foundation of our cherished values... To changing the shape of American morality ... You've smuck up on us through the backdoor. You're not strong enough to take us over by direct political action so you've chosen to drive us all crazy... I know when I'm being bushwhacked. (*SB-f* 205)

Niles was effective enough to dehistoricise the identities of Pablo and Louis against their supreme resistance. Like him they too became aware of being ahistorical bodies, displaced and acontextualised. Both Pablo and Louis became restless to go out of the apartment because they found the place a crazy and the case too complicated to be handled by them. When Paulette released an arrow directing toward the back of Niles it hit Pablo who immediately admitted, "This time they really got me... In the end we were not certain we could make neither head nor tail of the predicament. Whether or not we were destroyed from within or without now it makes no difference. There is only the reality of my dying!" (*SBF* 223). Louis, on the other hand, was attacked by an unseen face possessed by his own hand that tried to assassinate him. He became apologetic about his own American upbringing. He apologetically explained that it was not his fault being what he was:

> "Its Not my Fault! I Can't Healp It... I had to go to night school in my spare time to earn my diploma. The was took my time away I've shapnel acars on the back of my neck. Pieces of hard grenade still embedded in my knees. I'm entitled to a little dance music!.... (*SB-f* 213).

Ironically, Niles as a musician was already a mysterious figure for Louis and Pablo. They had problems understanding how he made a living. "Do composers get a salary"? Enquired Louis of his boss Pablo. Pablo answered him hesitontly, "Commissions whatever. He didn't earn much" (*SB-f* 195). Besides, the typical reason they could associate with a suicide was sudden material fall of the victim. They were further confused about the motive behind the suicide because "he was at the top of the bill. May be not as high up as you depict but pretty goddamn high up there. Why disappear when things are going so good. "It's crazy" (*SBF* 198). This mysterious figure turned out to be the force to deconstruct the entire edifice of cultural rationality to the extent that both Pablo and Louis found themselves on the verge of having lost all control over their body and mind. Like that of Niles they too started striving for assuming anonymity.

Niles disappeared to "remain mysterious. Anonymous" (*SB-f* 214), said Petrone. He was successful only partially, for he had to come back again to the old turf. He could escape a cultural ghetto dominated by "politicians", "gangsters", "rackets", "dope syndicates", "CIA" *et al.* Niles was more frightened by the insidious group which included "The Mind

Benders, The Chromatic Pursuaders, The Psychic Transfusions, The Cult mongers. All forms of ritualistic terrorism" (*SB-f* 210). He made a desperate attempt at self-obliteration but realised that to leave a "life" is not so easy "It's not the easiest thing in the world" (*SBF* 209). Niles could still smell the spoor of his own presence remained stuck in the places he left long before. Coming back to the old spot so he regretted that he should not have come back again. He, in fact, was a complete failure when it came to handling the reality that surrounded him. Pablo in one of his rare occasions of authentic judgement evaluated the issues that preceded and caused Niles's disappearance: "(Niles is) A victim of circumstances beyond his control... He bought off more than he could chew. He began dallying with power figures. He was sinking in a sea of confusion. His music was driving him mad". (*SB-f* 204)

Niles lost his mental equilibrium because even music went out of his control as he was not creating music but struggling to retain his legacy. He became a typical postmodern artist whose musical improvisations were "lasting for days on end" (*SBF* 204). The situation could best be defined in terms of George Steiner's view of "maximal impact and immediate obsolescence". He became a frantic and developed compulsive obsession to "reproduce" and "repeat" his tunes and had to be dragged from his piano and strapped to his bed; he was fed intravenously to keep him alive. He even lost his own voice. He could only utter some noises at varying pitch. He even became aware that he was possessed by his own gift. His voracious hunger for sound became a demon. He was possessed by multiple identities. He discovered other bodies inside "that lashed out without warning." "That took hold of him and swept him away. Each time with more and more violence..." (*SB-f* 204). It had its effect on his music which "turned into boring melodies" (*SBF* 209). He waited to be exorcised of the "demon" that took over his soul. He was thus always in a situation which Adorno would call "the state of unfreedom" in which no one has a liberated consciousness (see Lechte 95). Niles only had a reified appearance behind which lay the truth of the phantasmagoria of commodity production, and truth entails that human beings, despite what they might think, are unfree. This is because, they have restrictive forms of thought and action imposed upon them by the existing social conditions of capitalist production. They live, as Adorno says, in "an open air prison", and people adapt to the condition rather than oppose them. He had a feeling of freedom because he thought that the demon had left and he could go off on his own again. But he was soon reminded that he was not free. Freedom, as described by George Simmel, became a myth for Niles. Niles was warned that "he was still in danger. That as long as he'd be within their power he'd be all right. He'd be safe" (*SBF* 204). At this, as Pablo explained: "His mind would go back and forth between submissions and rebellion. His music was turning to pablum. Finally, he decided to leave them completely. And that's when they killed him." (*SB-f* 204).

Niles, after having killed, failed to redeem his self through his musical creations. He was completely defaced and was erased of any individual sign. He failed to locate his body, he could not even locate his self because he failed to identify the differences between him and the others. He was wondering at the pervasive presence of the other within him that he became untraceable even to himself. He would ask: "Are you inside me or outside me? Am I inside you? ... Am I buzzing away at your membranes? Your brainwaves. Driving you berserk? ... Destroying your ancient patterns? Or am I just like you? So exactly like you that we're exactly the same. So exactly that we are not even apart. Not even separate. Not even two things but just one. Only one. Indivisible."(*SB-f* 229)

Niles sought solitude to retrieve his creative self. He wanted to get rid of them all so that he could start al! over (*SBF* 210). He, therefore, wanted to reinvent himself by being dead so that the imposed identities too died with his death enabling him to be reborn with a clean slate. He wanted to be away from the elements that made false promises as Paulette tells Niles: "They 'Yes' you to death and then they slam you in the 'Tomb'" (*SBF* 227). After having made that attempt of escape, abortive though, Niles refused to go back home again. For him, his creative salvation lay in his being "Anonymous", "being on the streets; being "Already Dead." This anonymity could provide Niles one of the conditions of creativity.

For Maurice Blanchot, a major post-war critical thinker of France, any artistic work is anonymous, as it is the creative force of the work itself which effaces the presence of the author. The effacement of the author prioritises the work of art and thus establishes its singularity and significance. But, to remain significant on its own right has to subvert art institutions which might predetermine and stabilise the process of creativity by enclosing artistic exercise within a framework. Art, therefore, requires the artist to be in solitude, outside the impressionable range of institutions and individuals so that a work of art produced under such conditions can become an experience unique and exclusive (*See Lechte* 209).

Solitude is also a condition that forms an author's silence for work itself provides conditions for the writer's silence to take a shape. "The clean slate", the condition of being able to "wipe them all out" is what Paulette described as "perfect" (*SBF* 228). Niles wanted to regain his time when he could create totally a new kind of music. The kind of music that was terrifying for Pablo and Louis. Louis said nervously, "I am used to Tomy Dorsey, the Mills Brothers, Bary Goodman. All this free-flow stuff is disturbing to my inner depths. It leaves me feeling nauseous" (*SB-f* 213). He was satisfied being a Republican and an ardent follower of Eisenhower. ("I'm a Republican by nature! ... I'm not ashamed of that. Eisenhower was my main man!" (*SB-f* 213). Niles made attempts to be away from such commitments. He encountered his own image in the street, beckoning at him to come out of the window, the tomb, to put him at crucial moment of decision. His other ego on the street turned ahead and walked away and as he watched him going from behind the window he made a clean jump all the way to the bottom and the life went dancing out of the window (*SB-f* 221). The composer thus made a journey into a purely private aesthetic realm beyond the tangible reach of the community. Beyond the reach of his fans who are fanatics ("I'm a fan. A fanatic. I live for revenge", said Petrone (*SBF* 228). The solitude and anonymity rewarded Niles with music. Music he invented in order to drive off his loneliness: "I am afraid to be lonely. It's almost worse than dying ... That's the reason I invented music. It filled me up. I got so filled up that I could not go on. Now I gotta start over." (216)

But the tragedy lay in Niles's final submission. It resembled Lugi Pirandello's *When One is Somebody* (1933) in which the unnamed hero, an essayist, is permanently imprisoned in his own celebrity status. He must do everything as per public expectations. He finally turns into stone and as David J. deRose writes, became a "perfect unwavering monument to his artistic ideality, completely entombed by his public's expectations" (147). But Niles returned to the structured reality inhabited by Pablo and Louis without resolving any one of the dramatic answers nor by explaining the reasons of his return. "What's anyone waiting for? ... Am I dead or alive? Is this me, here, now? Are these questions or answers? ..." (*SB-f* 229). He returned to the so-called space of rational fixities only to disrupt its surface tranquillity by subverting this into a surreal, unanswerable, plausible territory.

The two plays reflect the perpetual conflict of artist with the oppressive reality of the new cultural grammar which forms the normative codes of or an artist to survive with. Both the artists Hoss and Niles, redeem their art through the rituals of self-destruction. Hoss destroys himself to become absolutely immune to all reductive mechanisims of the market forces and Niles, on the other hand, deconstructs himself to reach out to the spaces of pastoral innocence where he discovered his music. Both of them are the victims of their own legacy. When Hoss is made redundant through a simulated cultural product in the form of Crow, Niles is forced to simulate his own image over and over again. But both of them finally triumph over the repressive market mechanisms by subverting them through their silence and isolation.

Shepard profoundly disturbs the cultural complacency of his time when art is translocated to the territory of market, simulation, media hegemony, technical supremacy and cultural anarchy.

Notes and References

1. *Tooth of Crime* was first performed at the Open Space, London, on July 17, 1972, directed by Charles Marowitz.
2. *Sucide in B-Flat* was first produced at the Yale Repertory Theatre in New Haven, Connecticut on October 15, 1976, directed by Walt Jones.

Works Cited

Bauman, Zygmunt. *Postmodernity and its Discontents.* (1997).

Bigsby, C.W.E. *Modern American Drama: 1945-1990.* New York, Cambridge Cambridge University Press, 1992.

Clarke, David, Qtd. in Bauman. (1997). Ellington, Duke, Interview. "Sabata's Jazz:: An Argentinian Artist Looks at America's Music". Geoffrey C. Ward. *American Heritage*, October, 1995.

Ellington, Duke. Interview. " Sabata's Jazz: An argentanian artist looks at America's music" in Geoffrey C. ward. *American Heritage*, October, 1995.

Feingold, Michael. "Kleist and Shepard Flirt with Death", *The Village Voice*, November 15, 1976.

Firth, Simon, *Sound Effect: Youth Leisure and the Politics of Rock 'n' Roll.* New York; Pantheon, 1981.

Gregory, Lanier W. "The Killer's Ancvient Mask: Unity and Dualism in Shepard's *Tooth of Crime*". Toronto: *Modern Drama*, 36:1 (1993).

Lechte, John. "Theodor Adorno". *Fifty Key Contemporary Thinkers: From Structuralism to Postmodernity*, London: Routledge, 1996.

_____. "Maurice Blonchet." (1996).

Malkin, Jeanctte P. Verbal *Violence in Contemporary Drama: From Handke to Shepard.* Cambridge, New York: Cambridge University Press, 1992.

Marsalis, Wynton. Interview. "What is Jazz". Tony Scherman. Reprinted by Permission from *American Heritage*, October 1995. © Forbes Inc. 1995.

Mottram, Ron. *Inner Landscape*. Columbia: University of Missouri Press, 1984.

Patraka, Vivien M. & Mark Siegel. *Sam Shepard*. Boise State University, Boise Idaho, 1985.

Ponechen, Joseph. Review. "Yale Strikes Right Chord with Suicide in B-Flat". *Trumbull Times*, 1976.

Powe, Bruce. "Shepard's Way With Music". Toronto: *Modern Drama*, 36:1 (1993).

Shepard, Sam. "*Tooth of Crime*". *Sam Shepard Seven Plays*. New York: Bantam Books, 1981.

_____. *Suicide in B.Flat. Angel City and Other Plays*. New York: Urizen Books, 1977.

Wade, Leslie. *Sam Shepard and the American Theatre*. 1997.

Wetzsteon, Ross. Introduction. *Fool for Love and Other plays* (1988).

Wicke, Peter, *Rock Music: Culture, Aesthetic and Sociology*. Tr. Rachel Fogg.

Cambridge, NY: Cambridge UP, 1990, (Originally published in German as *Rock Music: Zur Asthetic und Sociologie eines Marrennediuns*, 1987).

6

Colonising Imagination: Hollywood and the Decentred Artists

Hollywood is a major cultural site where Sam Shepard locates his protagonists in conflict with the system. Shepard himself becomes a popular culture icon following his screen image. He has been very critical about Hollywood, yet he could not remain absolutely away from it. Like music, Hollywood too is an intimate experience for him. He made his first major motion picture appearance in *Days of Heaven* (1978) directed by Terence Malick. After that he acted in more than ten Hollywood movie and is a major Hollywood figure now. One of the most widely acclaimed commercially successful movie was *The Right Stuff* (1983) directed by Phil Kaufman. For his outstanding performance as Chuck Yeager, the pilot who could cross the barrier of time, Shepard earned an Oscar nomination in 1983. He was involved with Hollywood not only as an actor, but also as a screenplay writer. He wrote his first screenplay with Michaelangelo Antaonioni, *Zabriskie Point* (1968). His second major Hollywood screenplay was *Paris, Texas* (1984) which was directed by Wim Wenders. The movie was awarded the prestigious Palm d'Or in the Cannes Film Festival of 1984.

Despite being intimate to Hollywood, Shepard has always been cynical about the Hollywood experiences. Shepard describes his Hollywood experience as a "nightmare" (qtd. in Rosenberg, 11). The protagonists of the plays that the chapter would discuss would echo this Shepardian experience. The chapter takes three major plays of Shepard that deal with the Hollywood experience: *Angel City* (1976)[1], *Seduced* (1977)[2], and *True West* (1980)[3]. Hollywood is the setting of all these plays and Shepard makes a critique of Hollywood from the vantage of his personal experience.

The wild west and the Hollywood provide two contradictory geographical spaces intrinsically related to the mythic cultural desire of the *American Dream*. Hollywood is an integral part of the urban illusion of enlightening the universe which reinforces the perpetration of a dream into the mind of the masses that consequently translocates them to a psychic state of appropriation fundamentally based on self-deception. Shepard even said "movie audiences are dreamers" (qtd. in Goldberg 44). Hollywood, through gradual mastery over technology, evolved into a place for manufacturing dreams for mass consumption. It thus reifies an abstract creative experience into a lucrative marketable commodity. But Hollywood, for an artist, as Conard Wilcox describes it, is "the inner landscape of nightmare with its deep obsessions, dark compulsions and the outer geography of doom and apocalypse" (61). Mike Davies defines Hollywood as a "deracinated urban hell" (17).

Hollywood emerges against the backdrop of the cultural awareness of an empty space wherein the artificial invention of monuments and relics to prop up a façade of civilisational continuity has become a political necessity as America, as a nation, has continued to remain a metaphor of a future poised distantly, and Hollywood, therefore, ventures to affect a mechanism of breaking the dichotomies of this historico-cultural distance to evolve, what Jameson calls, "the phantasmagoric global American postmodernist culture". For Johannes Birringer this culture "is characterised by being a culture without a perspective." In Hollywood, artists are, as Tympany in *Angel City* puts it, "locked into the narrowest part of (their) dream machine" (40).

This are the modalities through which Hollywood colonises the artist's imagination. It entraps the subject in a space of perpetual monotony where the same products are circulated over and over again that eventually leads the subject to a situation in which the subject with a "deep sense of failure" (Shepard qtd. in Rlosen 26) fails to locate a space for himself.

Hollywood legitimises the process of appropriating the dominant ideology instead of formulating the idioms to question the system and evolving alternative discourses. Even when Shepard wanted two of his off beat plays, *Silent Tongues* and *Far North,* to produce into motion pictures, he did not find producers in Hollywood. Two French producers helped Shepard. A Hollywood film, Jim Collins points out, "is allegedly the dominant or hegemonic ideology writ in celluloid." (90) It never recognises the existence of the competing discourses within its domain. The result is the uncritical appropriation of the dominant discourse because it does not give any validity to the decentered universe, instead, Hollywood enforces a centric universe of the hegemonic ideology.

Hollywood is an institution for the systematic privileging of one language over others. Jim Luc Comelli explains Hollywood in Althusserian terms; "Because every film is part of the economic system, it is also part of the ideological system, for cinema and art are branches of ideology. None can escape...like the pieces in a jigsaw puzzle all have their allotted place. Cinema therefore fails to escape homogeneity." It remains a part of the uniform, identical mass culture where the artist becomes a terrible victim. Yet the artist, like the drum player, Tympani in Angel City, in almost Faustian fashion, is drawn to the Hollywood world. Lanx tells Tympani: "something drew you down here to us, something indescribable" (*AC* 31).

Shepard is known for his special fascination with Christopher Marlowe's *The Tragical history of Doctor Faustus.* "You know (sic) Doctor Faustus by Christopher Marlowe? I'd prefer it to Goethe's version because of Marlowe's incredible language" (qtd. in Cott 170). Shepard writes a play with a Faustian protagonist: *Man Fly*. Shepard's Doctor Faustus, Skeetz, is a poet in search of a muse who in desperation sells his soul to the Devil's emissary, Moustafo. Sam Shepard writes his very next play, *Angel City* (1976), in which this theme of selling of the soul by the artist for success reappears where the emissaries of Devil are the agencies of Hollywood.

In *Taper Literary Manager*, David Copelin, Director Robert Calhaun and writer Sam Shepard exchanged their views about Hollywood which formed the central setting of the play, *Angel City*. Copelin, however, defined the play not only as "melodrama about selling out" but more than that. The artist protagonist of the play, Rabbit Brown, is seen as aware of being attached to power as well as being repelled by it. Shepard described his experience of Hollywood as painful and torturous. "People here sink or swim without even knowing how it happens". The play, *Angel City,* is written by him from his own understanding and experience of Hollywood which is, as Shepard clarifies, "not to regurgitate it but to use it as a catalyst." Like Rabbit Brown, the artist protagonist, Shepard too got involved with Hollywood not only as an actor but also as a writer to join a project with Michaclangelo Antonioni at the age of around twenty-four for the film *Zabriskie Point,* what Shepard recalled as: "I was 24 and just wasted by the experience. It was like a nightmare". (qtd. in DeRore 80).

Toby Silverman Zinman describes the play as "about the grotesque ruthlessness of Hollywood, where characters named Wheeler deal for disasters and corruption is made visible, people run green and slimy, becoming the monsters they wanted to create" (514). Rabbit Brown, like that of Shepard experiences Hollywood as a terrible nightmare, who, in fact, encounters this in the form of the visceral degeneration of the producer from whose skin oozes slimy green viscous. The producer, who was to make a disaster to produce a blockbuster movie, himself transforms into a figure of apocalyptic degeneration. The play reaches its climax when the private ambition and thirst for power of Rabbit Brown itself turns out into a catastrophe as he fails to escape the identical doom like that of Wheeler, the producer. Rabbit, in almost Faustian desperation, makes vain attempts to rescue himself from his crude degeneration.

In the play Rabbit Brown becomes a voluntary prisoner like that of Skeetz (*Man Fly*) and Faustus to pursue fame and achieve recognition in exchange of his artistic ability. The play is an elegy on the demise of innocence epitomised by Rabbit Brown and Mrs Scoon.

Miss Scoons, in one of her trance states, unconsciously laments: "All innocence was now behind her. All dreams of the life of man free and unfettered as she once knew it was son the plains of Nebraska. Here was the hard care cement. *The concrete reality of the dreaming machine.* The terrifying destruction which faced her head on was now met by her own indivisible courage which she felt welling up from same deep primeval source which she knew not of. Suddenly the solution was clear. In her mind's eye was a simple equation. It appeared like a flashlight in a hooker's nightmare. Money equals power, equals protection, equals eternal life." (italics mine *AC* 18)

The system of Hollywood takes the artist as hostage as in *Geography of a Horse Dreamer* where Cody the man with a creative gift to dream horse numbers is chained to a bed by gangsters to force him to dream horse number, as in *Cowboy Mouth* where Slim is abducted to be made into a "Rock 'n' Roll, Jesus with a cowboy mouth" or Duke in *Melodrama Play* who is forced to write another successful chartbuster like "Prisoners, Get Up out of Your Home made Beds".

Sam Shepard, in one of his interviews to Carol Resen, talks about *Angel City*, as one where, "Artist/hero (is) exploited and devoured by movies". The artist is inescapably incarcerated by Hollywood's absolute illusions. About Hollywood's hegemonic ideological repression Shepard comments, "Hollywood is impervious to criticism. You cannot puncture the skin of that mechanism .... It's like steel armour. You can't even get next to it, because it's so completely locked up, guarded by the mechanism." (qtd. in Rosen 19)

Against the backdrop of Hollywood totalitarianism, the Hollywood aspirant with all his greed for success, is robbed off his imagination like Rabbit who becomes a conscious accomplice of Wheeler who epitomises the corruption of Hollywood. Rabbit Brown realises, "I've connived in the deepest cracks of the underground. Rubbed knuckles with the nastiest poets. Done the 'Rocky Mountain Back Step' in places where they've outlawed bubble gum."(*AC* 12)

The process that Rabbit is involved as artist is to disempower himself from even being able to communicate because it has systematically marginalised the language of his artistic self and put that outside the universe of communication prevalent in Hollywood. He realises that he could no longer remain an artist. Rabbit could no longer remain what Lanx called "a magician" and Miss Scoons "The messengers of God" (31). Instead, he realises what has he become, "I'm a stunt man. I fall off horses. I've done some sleight of hand. I've conjured a little bit. I collect a few myths, but this sounds like you need a chemical expert or something." (*AC* 15)

Lanx immediately endorses: "Exactly! A chemical expert. Very well put". (*AC* 15)

Shepard, like Nathaniel West, considers Hollywood images as luring and captivating but at the same time he makes his understanding emphatically clear that the dreams of Hollywood corrupt artist's imagination because Hollywood dreams, "In the profit sense of the word, of course" (*AC* 14). In order to assure the economic rationality of the project, Hollywood legitimises the postmodern mode of production that reduces art into a commodity. Wheeler stipulates the frameworks for creating this 'art object':

> [it] is not simply an act of terror but something which will in fact drive people right off the deep end. Leave them blithering in the aisles. Create mass hypnosis. Sucide. Auto destruction. Something which will open entirely new fads in sado-masochism. Penetrating every layer of their selves. Something which not only mirrors their own sense of doom but actually creates the possibility of it right there in front of them. It's our duty. We owe it to the public. For without the public we are nothing but a part of that public. We must stand apart, or another plane. We must rise to the challenge. We must help them devour themselves or be devoured by them. The time is ripe for this obliteration. We must rise to the occasion or be lost forever in a tidal wave of oblivion. (*AC* 15)

One of the reviews of *Angel City* by Dan Sullivan in *The Los Angeles Times View* (April 18, 1977), titled 'Surreal Trip', described the play in terms of the archetypal plot, Nice boy goes to Hollywood and becomes what he beholds ... The play plunges back and forth between fantasy and reality mixing them up to the point where the disaster movie where our producers are trying to get off the boards becomes the apocalypse they both fear and lick their lips for".

The involvement of the subject with the system becomes a ritual of self annihilation the way Tympani's position is described by Miss Scoons, "Frozen in the Act of Creation" (*AC* 19).

In the play, *Angel City*, Rabbit Brown and Miss Scoons abandon their innocence and willfully yield to the repressive ideological apparatuses operated by Wheeler. This inevitable subjugation of the artist to the apparatuses of the dominant order is a constant thematic concern in the plays of Shepard that deal with the issues relating to the creativity and creation of artists.

Cinema of Hollywood has deeper cultural significance. It is one of the most authentic expressions of the quintessential American fantasy. It is not a mere art, but a gorgeous reflection of the ideological American identity. As Lee says in *True West*: "In this business we make movies. American movies. Leave the films to the French" (30). Movie, in the American context, has greater semantic significance which reflect the figurations of the ideological illuminations of the national fantasy with such huge dimensions and grand operations that the subjects get blurred amidst the postmodern consciousness which is indistinguishable from the simulated images, spectacles, ideology. This aligning of the artist with the dominant ideological territory reinforces his translocation into a space of absolute vacuity. In his very act of entering the territory of dominant ideological topology, through a complex process of mechanised simulation, the artist soon makes an entry into a space of absolute absence.

Thus the condition of artistic existence is redefined within the new space. In case of Hollywood it means "Some little fantasy, some tiny little delusions that you've got tucked away. They'll pry it out of you. ...They'll feed off your hunger. They'll keep you jumping at carrots. And you'll keep jumping all the time you're jumping" (Tympany, *AC* 17). Through Hollywood the ideology transforms into a material entity in which the artist gets himself an illusion in concrete form. This concretisation of the ideological illusion is realised through the interrelationship between the subject and the system which affects, as Althusser would say, "imaginary representation of the real world" ("Ideology and Ideological" 164:1971).

Miss Scoons reflects it when she described her experience of the system:

> Here was the hard core cement. The concrete reality of the dreaming machine. The terrifying destruction which faced her head on was now met by her own indivisible courage which she felt welling up form some deep primeval source which she knew not of. Suddenly the solution was clear. In her mind's eye was a simple equation. It appeared like flashlight in a hooker's nightmare. 'Money equal power, equal protection, equal eternal life.' And with that she collapsed at the foot of La Cienaga.
> (*AC* 18)

The word 'ideology' was originally invented by Cabanis, Destutt de Tracy and their friends to define the theory of ideas (Althusser, 158), but in Shepard it turns out to be almost a Marxist ideological experience, that is, it dominates the mind of the man or the group of individuals. When most individuals or the group of individuals are easily dominated by the discourse, the artists try to resist it through their inherent capacity to remain as outsiders. The complex situational intricacies and the powerful apparatuses of the system are in combat with the artist, and the apparent failure to win as well as the resistance against defeat turns him into a being devoid of totality and a bricolage of fragments which Shepard himself has focused on in the beginning of his play *Angel City*. Shepard defines the "Character" in this context as a "fractured whole with bits and pieces of character flying off the central theme. In other words", continues Shepard, "move in terms of collage construction or jazz improvisation" (Note to the Actors, *AC* 6). Miss Scoons interrogates Wheeler about the authenticity of the act of self annihilation to emerge as what the public has imposed on them as an image. Wheeler assures: "Of course there is ... . We've to find that part of our own mind which corresponds to the masses. We're immune and contaminated at the same time" (*AC* 39). The realisation of the fact of being contaminated by Hollywood spurred one of the characters in Nathaniel West's *The Days of the Locust* to call Hollywood "the final dumping ground". When Wheeler here realises that he had lost in his gamble to turn his artistic enterprise into an industry of imagination, it turned out to be "Poisoned!" and "Putrified!" (*AC* 42). Rabbit endorses, "It's no business! It's a disease!" (*AC* 42).

The decrepit reality of Hollywood is physically represented by the *mise en scene* of the play such as the settings, costume, background music and other stage accessories which Wilcox has described as the inventive translation of disorder onto the stage ("Refiguring" 64). The incongruous assortment of stage paraphernalia like that of the producer's swivel chair, neon rectangle, timpani drums, the pale metamorphosis of light from black to yellow and the overbearing presence of darkness on stage and the characters like Rabbit who is dressed in detective suit, hat like Dick Tracy's and tennis shoes; the leather garbs of the secretaries with nun's habits, the English working garb of the drum players (white T-shirts, suspenders, baggy pants and heavy construction boots); wherein characters change, quite strangely, their roles as well as costumes, etc. This indeterminacy of physical reality is an echo of the ideological entropy which inherently features the quintessential Hollywood consciousness. Hollywood is not only a place of annihilation, but also a means of reappropriation.

Miss Scoons reveals her own simulation: "I look at the screen and I am the screen. I'm not me. I don't know who I am. I look at the movie and I am the movie. I am the star.... For days I am the star and not I am.... I look and I hate my life not being a star. I hate being myself in my life which is not a movie and never will be. I hate having to eat. Having to work. Having to sleep. Having to go to the bathroom.... Having to live in this body which isn't a star's body and all the time knowing that stars exist." (*AC* 21)

Miss Scoons, who represents countryside innocence, is unceremoniously drowned in almost an Yeatsian apocalypse. She desperately strives to abandon her real life in exchange the idealised life legitimised in the movies, where: "There are people doing nothing all their life except being in movies. Doing nothing but swimming and drinking and laughing and being driven to places full of potential. People never having to feel hot pavement or having to look at weeds growing through cracks in the city. People never having to look at the city square in the eyes. People living in dreams which are the same dreams I'm dreaming but never living." (*AC* 21)

The fragmental characters of Shepard are the prototypes of their corresponding landscape which too is fractured, disorganised that negates totality as well as integrity. This is mystic, alluring, dark and enigmatic. But the promise it makes to let the insiders forget the reality outside is what constantly attracts its victims. Tympany who enacts here the role of a chorus too, at times, represents the author's voice explaining the cinematic urge: "I just wanna go to the movies, Ma! I don't care about anything else!Just the movies! I don't care about school or homework or college, or jobs or marriage or kids or insurance or front lawns or mortgage or even the light of day! I don't care if never see the sun again, Ma! Just send me to the dark, dark movies!" (*AC* 24)

The conscious journey of the subjects into the dark zone of oblivion propels them to appropriate the discourse through the media which they have supposedly mastered to control and in the process they are actively engaged in thwarting the questions posed by the new entrants when it comes to redefining the status of an artist as well as the procedure of artistic creativity. Wheeler, who is one of the insiders of the system, dismisses Rabbit's claim of being an artist by saying, (Being a producer) "I'm in Demand! You're Dime A Dozen!" When Rabbit tries to assert his superiority by citing his creative capacity Wheeler described "Creation's a disease" (*AC* 45). The parameters for the producer are obviously different. This is 'auto-destructive' a 'mass hypnosis', created through hysterical media fed violence that has to configure an apocalyptic conflagration.

The individuals are displaced from their respective identities which forces the continuous fracture of their unpresentable identities. This eventually authenticates the fact of their being mere simulated stereotypes and their succumbing to the Hollywood hegemony. The subjects are fast reduced into unrecognisable nonentities. Miss Violet, a city prostitute in Rainer Fassbinders play *Garbage, the City & Death* comments: "From day to day the city is growing bigger. The people in it are growing smaller" (qtd. in Birringer 16). Similarly, the experience of Hollywood for the self conscious characters happen to be an encounter with a dehumanised, degraded space of suffering and destitution. The sight of Angel's City's spiritual degradation is found to have been reflected in a painting by Tod Heckett, called *The Burning of Los Angeles,* which captures the moment of a city's apocalyptic vision that traces the psychological journey of moving to the zones of the repressed, from Eros to Thanatos what Freud would define as "a society that is deeply in grip of the death drive". But the process has not only produced commodities, it also has reduced the supposed producers into commodities. Wheeler realises that his own presence emerges as an experience of eternal deference. He has been erased into an abstraction through a process of physical degeneration from whose body oozes the slimy green substance indicating the process of manufacturing movies which, as Wheeler claims, are inside his blood, churning around that tears him apart, "chewing (him) apart from inside out" (*AC* 43). In the process he even fails to make communication in physical/linguistic terms that could evoke any reciprocation. He finds himself amidst a world absolutely unintelligible and devoid of meaning. Rabbit Brown reminds Wheeler of the stark contrast of Hollywood fantasy with the reality which is not a mere "hanky, panky love story and romantically depicted apocalypse" (*AC* 51). This disclosure is a terrible threat to the very existence of Wheeler which turns out to be a 'hard core disaster' not only in case of the movie but to his sense of belonging to a milieu as well. Wheeler desperately urges Lanx to rescue him from the ongoing onslaughts of threats, but Rabbit makes the deadly blow by disclosing that they can't hear, they can't even see Wheeler for he has become an intangible entity through media simulation who, like the distant frontier of America, transforms into an ephemeral being constantly eluding physical authenticity that underlines the mutually agreed distancing dynamics of screen and spectators. Rabbit points out, "You are on the silver screen, buddy, you've been captured in celluloid and you'll never get out. All they are looking at is a moving picture show" (*AC* 52).

Despite Wheeler's frantic struggles to establish communication with Lanx and Miss Scoons, his torturously loud outcries remain absolutely inaudible which is a silent gesture for the onlookers who respond to Wheeler's desperation with smile and while chewing their popcorn (*AC* 52). And Rabbit discloses, "You're dead Wheeler. You're dead and gone" (52). Wheeler's claim of immortality soon transforms into a comic utterance, for in spite of his self-deceptive conviction of being alive in memories, he is ideally dead, a wreck of a corpse. He became a victim like the contemporary man whom Baudrillard, in his essay "Ecstasy of Communication", described as "the obscene prey of the world's obscenity"(132-133).

II

Shepard's next play *Seduced* (1978) portrays a Hollywood dream chaser who is literally seduced by Hollywood fantasies. Shepard here takes up a character who evolves into an imaginary entity like the figures on screen. Henry Michael Heckamore, the hero of the play, is totally devoured by the Hollywood fantasies.

Henry Michael Heckamore lives in a state of perpetual absence. His existence itself is based on the continual processes of Henry's compulsive dreams. Henry is seduced by his own dreams to accept the world of make believe as his reality. Arline Aisis writes in the review of the Trinity Hall Production of *Seduced*, "Dreams very often seduce us into believing that we have really done something, been somewhere, seen someone, when actually we haven't" ("Surrealistic Theater"). Henry Heckamore is physically antique who is "old to the point of looking ancient, body is thin and emaciated impression is a cross between a prisoner of war and an Indian fakir" (*Seduced* 233); who is almost naked, with white hair and long white beard and twisted finger nails and toe nails. He lives in a secluded island set in a third world, south of the border remove, somewhere in Mexico. There he makes attempts to be physically inaccessible to others as well as to himself. He is so obsessed with the images of his legend that he believes them to be non-diminutive, continual reality. He has a sparsely furnished well-controlled domicile where even nature assumes plasticity to be regulated as per Henry's wish. Two mechanically raised lush, well cared for potted palm trees about seven feet tall are the first things that Henry wants to be properly placed and well positioned. The room is distinguished by a set of velour drapes reflecting the recluse's partitioned existence and his distance from the world beyond. His obsession with seclusion is so acute that he even cannot tolerate daylight. So he moves only at night. It is darkness that allows him to accomplish his escapes from the world of stark actuality. He prefers black, "It's pitch black out here. Perfect. Perfect for escape" (275). Henry's mission is to make an escape in absolute terms.

The character of Henry Heckamore is admittedly modelled on Howard Hughes, the business tycoon who ended his life in mysterious seclusion. Henry Heckamore is a hermit, like Hughes, an aeronautic entrepreneur and a successful Hollywood producer. During the prime of Henry's time he attained all there is to take from life. He exemplifies America's popular notion of material success – "a surplus of women, war glory, material landslides" (Aisis). "That the capacity for joy has gone dry. His soul is a void, his mind is muddled. What is left of the man is only breath, bones and skin, some of which are not even his". It is, ironically, his own legendary power that enslaves him.

The appellation 'Heckamore' refers to a rope device to break horses. His name refers to Henry's own paradox. He, at one point of time, mounted and mastered the world but now he is in bouts of delusion and compulsive withdrawal which have rendered him broken. He eventually became, what Leslie Wade would, "a sullen and isolated misanthrope" (85). Henry's awareness of his own degeneration makes him fearful of the 'world' which he can no longer control. Hence, he finds the same world that he used to control as, "Wild. Undominated. Ravenous for the likes of us. Ready to gobble us up at the drop of a hat. We can't allow penetration. Not at any cost. Whatever the price we have to pay it to ensure our community. You have to ensure that for me Ravel. It's in your hands." (*Seduced* 254)

Henry is not only afraid of the world, he fears even the national space where he had his moments of glory. He realises that it was not he who had done the things, but it was through him that things had been done. Through him they gratified there own desires, "I'm the demon they invented. Everything they ever aspired to. The nightmare of the nation! .... I'm dead to the world but I never been born." (*Seduced* 275)

Henry is an invention of the media that instigated him to have the day dreams of success, glamour, fame which ultimately seduced him into becoming someone else. And he eventually is doomed to become the living entity of the nation's nightmare. America becomes an alien space for Henry where he cannot even dare fall ill, "This country is not fit for a man to fall ill in. There ought a' be a law against falling ill in a foreign country. A man's got a right to die in his homeland." (*Seduced* 270)

He admonishes Raul when he puts forward the proposal to fly over America in day time for he has not seen it for the last ten years. Henry warns by disclosing his own experience about America, "Nothing's changed. I guarantee it. All it would do is tempt you. Fill you with a lot a' aching. Desire again. Desire all over the place. Land of Lust." (*Seduced* 238)

It is this lust that has made Henry invisible. This has rendered him an entity devoid of his self, his soul. That is the reason Raul cannot see Henry's soul because this is that "unseen part that is thoroughly ravaged, beyond recognition." (239)

Henry, the physical recluse, in order to gain supreme control over his private reality, goes for the selective evocation of his lost past through a process which he is confident of manipulating as per his needs. Henry too reflects the concern of Lanx as in *Angel City* who admitted, "My power lies in manipulation. If no one is manipulated, there I'm sunk" (*AC* 33). Here, however, Henry wants to manipulate his reality, so he insulates not only the place he lives in but also himself from the outside world. "Nothing from out there comes in here! Not sun not moon, not sound, not nothing!" (*Seduced* 249). Henry has incarcerated himself almost in an antiseptic tomb where nothing from outside touches him. His previous existence into that outside world has been metaphorically described to be an experience of rape. There is mutual repulsion between Henry and the world, "It is a mutual arrangement. I don't touch it, it doesn't touch me. That's what happens when you rape something .... After that you don't touch. There's a repulsion between both sides." (*Seduced* 251)

For Henry, the total history of the immediate past is a repulsive aftermath. Hence, he takes pain to recreate the selective set of events that would ensure the continuation of his seductive dreams of the past. In order to reinvent the mystery that enshrouded him, he invites two sultry Hollywood sirens, Luna and Miami, to visit him. They appear in front of Henry directly from their past without ageing. Henry, the fantasist who has been preferring "images to acts and appearances to actualities" (Mottram 28), asks the girls to tell him about life which, in fact, he never experienced. He makes a final attempt to know, at least, about life before his complete obliteration. He does not want to have the sensation of it in the form of a metaphorical abstraction but he wants to experience it in absolutely concrete and physical form (smell, taste and sound of life). He aspires to have a physical contact. Besides, he wants to experience the tangibility the two girl friends who themselves are the inventions of his own imagination and whose movements are also controlled by himself, whom he wants to appear "Like visions. Like moving pictures." He wants them to appear in the form of beauty idealised, refined and flawless. That is what Henry is accustomed to – distilled reality. Like movies. He is comfortable with images not with physical immediacy.

Ron Mottram considers Henry as an artist because of his desire to manipulate and his preference for images though he is cut off from the areas of experience that is essential to the artist or, at least, to Shepard's conception of artist (for Shepard artist must have a sense of belongingness, must have roots).

Leslie Wade describes Henry as a "fantasist, a version of the artist who seeks the farthest outpost of imagination" (85-86).

Paradoxically, Henry's power lies not in his propinquity to his immediate reality. He is protected by the ambiguity of his existence. His mysterious disappearance ensures the enigma that he painstakingly built up around himself. It is the lack of knowledge about Henry that makes others fearful about him. Henry is well aware of this; therefore, he does not want to demystify his existential reality:

> Some even think I'm dead. Others don't know. Most others don't know. That's the best of all. Keeping them all in the dark. That's the best... . Worst is invisible. They know that. That's why they fear me. They can't put a finger on me. A stab on the dark.... They comb the cities for me. Little American towns. Fortunes are spent on hired assassins. Presidents fear me. International Secret Agencies. Internal revenues. Secretaries of Defence. Mobsters. Gang lords. Dictators. Insurance Detectives. None of them can touch me. None of them. (*Seduced* 251)

When Luna urges Henry to touch her, he discloses, he 'can't'. Being a product of the American mass media and consumerism, He becomes a veritable slave of marketing manipulation and simulation that shuts him round. His obsessive paranoia is vividly reflected by his neurotic act of spreading Kleenex sheets over his entire body. He accomplishes consumerist rituals that give him an illusion of satisfaction – the satisfaction of being possessed and controlled. He thus becomes a perfect product of that culture what he calls "Nightmare of the nation". Eventually it is not he who seduced the culture with his own powerful inventions (his planes, his hotels, his movies), rather he himself has been seduced by the dreams about his own mythology through which he relapsed into a state of obliteration. "He has become", as David J. De Rose says, "a living metaphor of the great American dream of supreme wealth and power" (89). But in the process he lost a vital aspect—freedom. As an attempt to regain control over himself he tries to reinvent his invisibility to subvert the attempts of the state agencies to erase his metaphysics of presence. Paradoxically, it is his invisibility that signifies his presence.

His visibility would destabilise the image that he stands for. It is the modified and unreal shadow of his that replaces his real existence. He even believes the abstract notion about himself to be the truth and all other truth and realities as nonexistent. He would celebrate his own death, because even death cannot destroy him, for the physical Henry is already dead. He survives beyond his mortal remains. "I'm dead to the world but I never been born" (278). He is aware of the process that transformed him into a fictive reality, a made—up entity. But in private he discovers that he has his own pastoral nostalgia. The nostalgia about the west and the myths associated with it. For him his reality belongs to Texas:

> Texas. That's the last time I lived on this earth. Texas. I disappeared myself into another shape. Another body. I made myself up... . I happened in a second, in a flash. I was taken by the dream and all the time I thought I was taking it. It was a sudden seduction. Abrupt. Almost like rape. You could call it rape. I gave myself up. Sold it all down the river. (*Seduced* 174)

Henry admits, he sold his soul like Faustus and in a flash he is robbed off his soul. Now even his blood is not his own. He even does not know whose body he is in. He recalls his total subjugation to an unreal self-identity based on lies. His reality is a product that reflects the bankruptcy of corporate capitalism. He is no longer powerful to assert anything different for it is not the mere destruction of subjectivity as the historical circumstances have also transformed the subject itself. He is beyond any possibility of regaining his lost selfhood which had its home in Pastoral Texas.

In his life, truth had only a marginal value when he himself is a simulacra, invented by the corporate world's apparatuses of seduction. Miami fumbles to narrate an imaginary story about her Las Vegas experience and Luna is asked to tell the same story. Luna protests, "But That's her story" (265). But for Henry it is not authenticity but the convincing manipulation that is what counts. He becomes an inseparable part of the mechanisms of manipulation which he fatally interpellates at the expense of his private rationality. About the difference of stories and their authenticity, he comments, "What difference does it make? It's a good story. One story is as good as another. It's all in the way you tell it. That's what counts. That's what makes the difference." (*Seduced* 265)

Henry is conditioned to react to the simulated reality. Howard Hughes too was said to have watched the same movie over and over again because he knew that they would not change. Similarly, Henry too regulates the events of life covering all "Variables". He distrusts physical existence. He is a corpse, as the world outside knows him as a pilot who, wearing his clothes, crashed over Nebraska. He attempts a retreat to his past through the "played out" narrative by the seductive women of his past who are his "last link" to the world; his very "last possibility ... for remembering. For bringing something back" (262). He needed women, "woman's version" (50). He finds women to be his last resort to regain power. He even faints at the incorrigible power of feminine seduction:

> Your femaleness. It's an awesome power .... It's not only you it's a force. With men I was always a master. They'd lick my heels. Men become dogs in a second. It's the female that's dangerous. Uncontrollable. Cat like .... At the front door to death I needed women! Women to fill me up. To case me into other world. To see me across. To bring me ecstasy and salvation. Don't let me fall! Don't ever let me fall. (Henry Collapses). (*Seduced* 250/51)

But he collapses in the midst of the process of attaining what he said "salvation" (251) through his failed attempts to orchestrate a moment of cohesion.

After having failed to reach at any rapprochement with his ghost lovers he wishes to return to America, the place of his origin, with a bid to regulate his own historical courses. He wants to go back to that space from where he disappeared. His nostalgic journey takes him to the space that never had any communion with the people that lived there. It was a space of dissociated totality, a place of the entities divorced from each other. That was a place "Flat, barren. Wasted as far as eyes could take in enormous country. Primitive. Screaming with hostility toward man .... As though men didn't belong there. As though men were a joke in the face of it"(271).

This is the place where Henry encountered the laughter of rattle snakes and coyotes: Cactus stabbing the blue air. Miles of hit and wind and red cock where nothing grew but the sand and far off invisible little man were huddled against it in cities. In tiny towns. In organisations. Protected (where) the whole world of men (was) pathetic. Sad, demented little morans moving in circles. Always in some circles. Always away from the truth. Getting smaller and smaller until they finally disappeared. (*Seduced* 271)

Henry captures the image of civilisation that the post-industrial west produced; of which he too is an integral part. With his destroyed subjectivity the only thing that remains substantial for his is "Air". He even writes his will, making Raul as the heir to his holdings, not on paper but in air. ("Air is the only thing that'll last forever" 271). In the process of executing the will in air Henry recounts the place and the process of his disappearance. ("I disappeared in a dream" 274). Like Niles in *Suicide in B-flat* he disappeared from his own persona. But he admits that he has been seduced, that his life has been a chasing of a mirage. Recognising his damned condition he is infused with a 'Mephistophilean energy' (Wade, 86). He assumes his chair as though it were a cockpit and embarks upon a final nefarious flight to Las Vegas which he saw as "glowing in the dark" (275). He finally is consciously blurred with his faceless anonymity. His was "A face. A name. No one will ever know for sure...Invisible. A ghost in the land. No sound. A phantom. They'll never get rid of." (275)

He becomes an image that cannot even be destroyed. His destruction is possible only through the destruction of the system that 'invented' him. Raul fires at him repeatedly, but bullets have no effects, because he has transcended his physicality. He is an entity that has turned into a legend of a hidden power and manipulation, raped by a dream and eventually becomes the "nightmare of the nation." Ron Mottram calls him "the end product of an aspiration for power and success, the ultimate American" (130). He can move anywhere he wants to, "Freer than life" (276). His body is gone. Nothing can see him. Henry utters, "I'm dead to the world but I never been born." He rises up in menacing triumph, a phoenix-like figure before whom Raul, the representative of the corporate culture, "collapses in a gesture of supplication" (276).

III

True West (1980) follows the author's shift to a new zone of American experience—nostalgia for a family. Shepard focuses more on the private universe of individuals menaced by the constant apprehension of being isolated from the family unit and being devoid of a sense of Home. The theme is of central concern in his *Buried Child* (1978) and *Curse of the Starving Class* (1977). *True West* is mostly seen as part of Shepard's "family trilogy".

The present study would, however, look at the play in relation to the issues that this study is concerned with. The two brothers, Lee and Austin, in the play are engaged in creative writing—Hollywood screenplays. The play captures the moment of two men's chase for a personal image that is provisionally translated as 'true west'. But this journey is accompanied by their perpetual awareness of having taken a tour toward an uncertain destination. The uncertainty prompts the two brothers to go for role reversals. Austin, the well set, self-complacent Hollywood screenplay writer, takes on the role of his Bohemian brother, Lee, a petty burglar and a scrounge of a fellow who lives in the desert with a dog. Lee, on the other hand, in a bid to abandon his native identity, takes up the role of his brother and starts writing a screenplay which he claims to be the story of true life. Austin, on the contrary, reduces himself into a petty thief breaking into the neighborhood to steal toasters. The act, apparently, provides Austin a peculiar sense of freedom that enables him to situate himself outside the claustrophobic world of urban propriety.

Lynda Hart in her book *Sam Shepard's Metaphorical Stages* (1987) describes the play as the struggle between rugged individualist of the frontier against the urban socialite which reflects, according to her, Shepard's own dissenting voice that has rebelled against the restrictions of urban life to defiantly, and often nostalgically, assert the claims of freedom and adventure embodied in the myth of the American West (88). Shepard, however, is concerned with other crucial aspects as well. As Wendy Lesser in his review underlines, the play also focuses on the degree to which the actual life of the old-time-West has been sentimentalised and corrupted by Hollywood's illusions. "In Shepard's imagery," writes Lesser, "this aesthetic corruption finds a physical counterpart in the encounter of one wild landscape by a spreading sunbelt suburbia" (19). On a broader conversation, Shepard is concerned with the general impact of Hollywood on America's process of creating fiction. Words like 'true', 'authentic' seem to become titular entities unless the work is approved by Hollywood—the aesthetic authority, represented in the play by Saul Kimmer.

The play discloses the tragic entrapment of the creative artist, the social validity of whose work is entirely dependent on the whims of the forces like Saul Kimmer. For Sam Shepard himself, Hollywood is a 'giant machinery'. Hollywood even absorbs the creative idiosyncrasy of Antonioni with whom Shepard was engaged as a screenplay writer for *Zabriskie Point* (1968). Shepard admits that the experience of working with Antonioni was a "nightmare" because "Hollywood problems and Big Business problems got in the way." He points out "There is no way you can work on a major motion picture without the producer having the last say on what's going to be in the film" (qtd. in Copelin, p. G).

Saul Kimmer in *True West* enjoys this invisible power which authorises him to accept or reject a script absolutely on the ground of his private taste and fancy. In a minute, he can turn Austin into just a nobody by rejecting his proposal and accepting Lee's script instead over a golf club by offering him a ridiculously huge sum of money as advance. This dramatic turn around of events beckons the ambitious desires of individuals and Lee is also lured by this mystery and promise. Shepard observes, "a lot of people sink or swim in it (Hollywood) without knowing how it happens, without knowing how you find yourself in a studio office, and without knowing how there you become involved in your first draft" (qtd. in Copelin). He underlines the problematics of being a Hollywood screenplay writer. As a playwright one could find an intimate communion with himself but as a screenplay writer one has to collaborate with dozens of people which is a completely opposite way of working" (qtd. in Copelin). He calls Hollywood 'a dead set' and most of the time what one gets, according to him, is a 'big podge'. Lee's so called true-to-life story is one such pastiche which Saul Kimmer attests as authentic by referring to some vague elements of the story to justify his claim. Kimmer says "(The story) has the ring of truth". Austin dismisses him with a laughter and asks "Why ? Because it got horses? Because it got grown up men acting like little boys?" Kimmer fumbles: "Something about the land. Your brother is speaking from experience." Even Austin claims that his stories were also from his experience. Kimmer defends himself by arguing, "But nobody's interested in love these days, Austin. Let's face it" (35). But Austin's source of authenticity as a counterpoint to Saul Kimmer's is equally vulnerable and naïve.

Austin makes a desperate attempt to outweigh Kimmer's claim by frantically arguing with almost boyish naivety, "(Lee) has been camped out on the desert for three months. Talking to cactus. What's he know about what people wanna see on the screen! I drive on the freeway everyday. I swallow the smog. I watch the news in colour. I shop in the safeway. I'm the one who's in touch! Not him!" (*TW* 35).

Austin, in fact, tragically fails to understand that his artistic paradigm may not be the one that Hollywood appreciates. Hollywood has its own modalities of aesthetics which are absolute in its own right. As Shepard once remarked on Hollywood's needs, "They want jokes. They want clever language, things like that. I don't think that any writer in his mind, who wants to write for himself, would try to write for the movies" (qtd. in Copelin). Hollywood is engaged in the creation of the objects of illusion to cater to the audience who are also, as Shepard says, 'dreamers'. Austin obviously fails to be patronised by a Hollywood producer for he represents a rational view. He is Harvard educated, orderly and intellectual. He believes in having a reward for hard work and punishment for misbehaviour. He is, as Wendy Lesser puts it, "a bit too restricted but safe". Lee is a complete contrast to what Austin stands for. He is translucent weirdo. His is a world which is messy, drunken, fragmented, irresponsible, violent, filled with lies, half truth and hard truths. Lee is almost an invention created by Hollywood's own need. He is the psychological other of Austin's rational self. Lee registered natural triumph where Austin failed. But Lee's freedom too is restricted within the territory demarcated by Hollywood.

The rejection of Austin's story by Saul Kimmer is emblematic of the course that work of art is to take. That it is not the artist who is empowered to endorse his own work but the power lies at a different centre that determines art's validity.

The second act depicts the gradual transformation of the Austin the artist and his steady approximation of the geography to which Lee belongs. Austin decides to abandon his private prairie and begs Lee to take him to the desert. Ironically, Austin endorses the authenticity of Lee's plot where two cowboys chase each other down the desert toward an uncertain destination—the 'Tornado Country'. But Austin describes Lee's story, to his chagrin, as a contrived one because two guys are made to chase each other in bizarre coincidental circumstances. The two guys are on tracks with 'goosenecks' (cattle trailer as explained by Lee, 20) where they have got their horses saddled up. The first guy, the one in front, realises that he is chased by the one who has illicit relationship with his wife. Both of them are out of gas and are bound to mount their horses to chase each other. Lee, however, dismisses Austin's reservation about the real life value of such a story. He insists that this is what exactly happens in his story, his "true-to-life-western". He ends the outline of his story with the description that turns out to be almost oracular assertions of what actually happens between the two brothers. The two brothers' survival in uncertain space prompts them to exchange their locations only to end up being nowhere.

Lee's closing of the outline betrays their own aporia: "So, they take off after each other, straight into an endless black prairie. The sun is just coming down and they can feel the night on their backs. What they don't know each one of them is afraid. And they keep ridin' like that straight into the night. Not knowing. And the one who's chasing doesn't know where the other one is taking him. And the one who's being chased doesn't know where he's going" (*TW* 27).

But Lee is handicapped as he requires Austin's help to write his story. Saul Kimmer's acceptance of the story makes Lee aware of his formal entry into a different world where instinctive existence is out of question. He makes an agreement with Austin that he would take Austin to the desert if he writes the story for him.

Austin responds mockingly: "Oh, now you're having a little doubt, huh? What happened ? the pressure is on boy. This is it. You gotta come up with it now. You don't come up with a winner on your first time out they just cut your head off. They don't give you a second chance ya' know." (*TW* 40).

Lee is almost trapped by the 'Hollywood blood-money' (*TW* 8). He mocks at Austin's work as 'dumb fuckin' line and he wonders "you get paid for dreamin' up a line like that?" (*TW* 8) But what Lee himself creates, says Austin, are the characters from his boyhood fantasies: "the illusions of characters – fantasies of a long host boyhood!" (*TW* 40). Austin then claims he has a "true story", the story of his father. He narrates the story of his father's losing all his teeth in a bag of American Chop Suey.

The old man started losing his real teeth one every morning, so he went to a Mexican dentist to 'yank' his teeth and the dentist took away all his remaining teeth and his money. Finally, he put the teeth in a doggie bag in which he was carrying Chop Suey from a restaurant. He left the bag in one of the bars that he went to get Austin introduced to some of his old friends. He left the bag there and they could not find the bag and he could not get those teeth back. Ironically, it is the old man's search for his past connection that caused him to lose all his teeth. This is what Austin call "The true story. True to life." (*TW* 42).

The penalty that Austin had to pay for his successful living in the city appears to be too costly for him. He, therefore, wishes to go to the desert where he expects to find the space of lost innocence. The cityspace for him is empty, barren and lifeless. He takes a look at his own urban existence and finds: "There's nothing here. There never was. When we were kids here it was different. There was a life here then. But now – I keep comin' down here thinking it's the fifties or something. I keep finding myself getting off the freeway at familiar landmarks that turn out to be unfamiliar. On the way to appointments wondering down streets. I thought I recognised, that turn out to be replicas of streets I remember. Streets I misremember streets I can't tell if I lived on or saw in a postcard. Fields don't ever exist anymore.... There's nothing real down here, Lee. Least of all me." (*TW* 49).

Through a series of accusations and confessions the two brothers come to agree with each other's proposals in a fleeting moment of fraternal bonding. The bonding grows through the exchange of power symbolised by Austin's car. It is the car that demarcates the identities of the two brothers. Lee wants to borrow Austin's car and Austin is torn between giving up his car and keeping it to himself. The keys move back and forth between the two brothers indicating what Wendy Lesser calls, "the shift of power between them and alternately heightening and releasing the sense of enclosure". Lee now wants to get away from the world he thought made up of real objects, 'something authentic' and not 'plastics' (*TW* 58). He finds the cityspace as the breeding ground of insanes. He expresses the desperation:

> I'm clearin' outa' here once and for all. All this town does is drive a man insane. Look what it's done to Austin there. I'm not lettin' that happen to me. Sell myself down the river. No Sir, I'd rather be a hundred miles from nowhere than let that happen to me. (TW 57)

Survival in the city (Hollywood) is only based on illusions constructed in the guise of art. Shepard makes this point as to how much the subjects really depend on the illusions created by art, by rituals, by language. Shepard understands, writes Wendy Lesser, as do all good playwrights, that those illusions may well be our only access to reality. Shepard carefully deconstructs the factors that hold the social fabric intact. He lampoons Hollywood as well as questions the authenticity of the West. The American myths in the play is cuddled in pop fantasies. Shepard is both appalled and fascinated by this process which accentuates the plays' ambivalence –the ambiguous power. The two brothers in the play even become a kind of "Pop Cain Abel" (Jack Kroll). Their mother's retreat to Alaska, the last possible frontier of the West, failed to provide the solace she expected there. "It was the worst feeling being up there. In Alaska, staring out a window. I never felt so desperate before" (59). Mom shares her experience with Austin. She comes back from Alaska to meet Picasso whom she thought was still alive. She returns to the home now unfamiliar with unwatered plants and the unexpected arrival of her elder son with whom Austin is engaged in a fight. "I can't stay here. This is worse than being homeless" 59.

The two brothers also find the home unlivable and finally disappear from there to merge in the desert against the fading prowling of coyotes. They, through violence, discover the process of creation which they didn't know before. They exchange their respective aesthetic abilities. This aesthetic exchange, says James C. McKelley, sparks off a "corresponding ontological exchange, setting in motion a chase between two contraries over the internal frontier of a shared identity". (298). These opposing principles of creativity are interdependent on each other.

But then artistic union requires a freedom for an untrammeled contact with the landscape of human exigency and an integration with "the common endeavour of human civilisation" (McKelley 299). This is how they can be on 'intimate terms' with the 'prairie' (*TW* 52). The phrase 'intimate terms' of Austin is found provocative by Lee. The phrase could provide an articulate expression to Lee's own aesthetic longing: "Sounds original now. "Intimate terms". That's good. Okay. Now, you are cooking! That has a real ring to it." (*TW* 52)

They want to be on 'intimate terms' with their aesthetic geography as they yearn to rediscover themselves in a space like that of the foothills of Saint Gabriel mountains, where Lee finds, "a sweet kinda' suburban silence.... Like a paradise. Kind's place that sorta' kill you inside. Kinda' place you wish you sorta' get up in." (*TW* 12)

The artists in these plays are exposed to a world torn between the beauty of their private vision and the ugliness of reality. They emerge as cultural nomads in search of an undefined habitat.

Lee in *True West*, the original nomad, comes out of his native habitat—the desert—when Austin leaves his comfortable urban domicile to rediscover his lost identity in the open space of the West. The desert is the space where the fixities of identities can be perpetually erased. Edmond Jabes writes: "in the desert there are no avenues, no boulevards, no blind alleys and no streets. Only here and there fragmentary imprints of steps quickly effaced and denied" (39). The desert, the address of Lee, provides a unique experience of virtual arrival validating the wandering of yesterday as a purposeful venture. On the other hand, for Lee, home reflects the point of his supposed arrival which is at the same time pregnant with the possibility of new departure.

In the course of role reversal, Lee unlike Rabbit Brown (*Angel City*) and Henry Hackamore (*Seduced)* becomes, what Zygmunt Bauman would call, an aspiring 'Parvenu' and Austin manifests his desire to reduce himself into a 'pariah'. Bauman defines parvenu as an "arriviste, someone already in, but not quite of the place, an aspiring resident without a residence permit" (72). He is someone who wants to forget the past and wish away the future and the older tenants dislike him because he awakens the memories and premonitions which they struggle hard to put to sleep (Zygmunt Bauman, 1997).

The artists who are drawn to the dazzled wonder of Hollywood are not always privileged to be a 'parvenu'. Like Austin, Rabbit Brown in *Angel City* and Henry Heekamore in *Seduced* are devoured by the system to the point that they can no longer retreat. Their identities are effaced. Hannah Arendt notes, when a subject is forced to transform identity by the system, he is even denied the right to be (himself) in anything and in any moment" (Qtd. in Bauman 74).

The artists in these plays are classic chasers of a mirage. They voluntarily exchange their respective spaces and roles by being allured by the majestic promises shimmering at the end of the tunnel. Rabbit Brown in *Angel City* passionately justifies his being seduced by Hollywood: "Millions seeing the same story..... Replacing their books. Replacing their families. Replacing religion, politics, art conversation. Replacing their minds. And I ask myself, how can I stay immune ? How can I keep distance from a machine like that?" (*AC* 13).

They finally end up being at artificial homelands what Bauman describes as 'hallucinations at best, vicious delusions at worst" (78).

But in the course of their search for a native space Lee and Austin in *True West* regain almost a tribal wisdom and urgency to trace a traditional space of belongingness. A place which is "authentic", "someone" which can keep (them) "in touch" (*TW* 56). But, paradoxically, their search for a space to relive their past experience in retrospect has only accentuated the absolute disappearance of the tradition and the locale that was supposed to cater a space of belongingness.

Lee is horrified to live in the world of Austin where identities can be adopted and discarded like disposable objects. The terrifying thing of the new situation is that all diligent work may prove to be in vain. This for Lee is a world of 'plastics'. Miss Scoons in *Angel City* describes the world where "one minute its good, the next minute its garbage" (*AC* 19).

The artists are terrible victims of Hollywood's devastating impact. Hollywood subjugates them to the extent of reducing the artists into, as Henry said in *Seduced*, 'demons". However, Shepard's next major Hollywood play, *True West,* ends with an optimistic note as the artists are able to, at least, undertake a journey work towards an imaginary destination that is not a part of the simulated cultural map of Hollywood. When Rabbit Brown, Wheeler, Miss Scoons, Lanx and Tympani are all devoured by the Hollywood machine while making a Hollywood movie, ironically titled as *Fronzen in the Act of Creation*, Henry Heckamore in *Seduced* becomes a shadow of his own simulated image; Lee and Austin in *True West* indicate that they could make a timely exit from the site before being annihilated. This possibility of escape, perhaps, emboldened Shepard to keep on flirting with Hollywood as an actor. Like Lee, he knows the route to escape.

Notes and References

1. *Angel City* was first produced at the Magic Theatre, San Francisco, on July 2, 1976, directed by Shepard himself.
2. *Seduced* was first produced at the American Place Theatre in New York. It was directed by Jack Gelber.
3. *True West* was first performed at the Magic Theatre, San Francisco on July 10, 1980.

Works Cited

Aissis, Arline. Review of *Seduced*. Dit. Adrian Hall, Trinity Square Reportory Co., "Providence. Surrealistic Theatre is seducing". (Prof. Jasbin Jain's News Clipping File). n.p.

Althusser, Louis. "Ideology and Ideological State Apparatuses (Notes Toward an Investigation)" in *Lenin and Philosophy and Other Essays*. Trans. Bren Brewster. London: New Left Books, 1971.

Baudrilliard, Jean. "The Ecstasy of Communication". Trans. John Johnston. *The Anti-Aesthetic*. Ed. Hall Foster. Port Townsend. Washington: Bay Press, 1983.

Bauman, Zygmunt. *Postmodernity and Its Discontents*. New York: New York University, 1997.

Birringer, Johannes. *Theatre, Theory, Postmodernism*. Indianapolis: Indianapolis University Press, 1991.

Collins, Jim. *Uncommon Cultures: Popular Culture & Postmodernism*. New York: Routledge.

Comolli, Jean Luc and Jean Narboni. "Cinema, Ideology, Criticism". *Movies and Methods*, Vol. I. Ed. Bill Nichols. California: Berkley University of California Press, 1976.

Copelin, David. Interview. "From Theatre to Film and Back". Interview of Sam Shepard and Robert Calhoun, *Taper Literature Magazine* (n.d.) D-H.

Cott, Jonathan, Qtd. in Patrick J. Fennel. "Shepard's Lost Sheep." Sam *Shepard: A Case Book*. Ed. King Kimball. NY: Garland, 1988.

Davies, Mike. "City of Quartz: Excavating the Future in L.A." New York: 1990. (qtd. in Wilcox, "What is the Day of the Locust and Shepard's Angel City: Refiguring L.A Noir", *Modern Drama* 36:1 (1993) 61-75.

De Rose, David J. *Sam Shepard*. New York: Tawane Publishers, 1982.

Goldberg, Robert. "Off Off Broadway's Street Cowboy". Rolling Stone's College Paper, October 1980.

Hart, Lynda. *Sam Shepard's Metaphoric Stages*. New York, London: Green Press, 1987.

Hoeper, Jeffrey D. "Cain, Canaanites and Philistines in Sam Shepard's True West, *Modern Drama* 36:1 (1993).

Jabes, Edmund. "Un etranger avee, saus le bras, un livre du petiti format" (Paris: Gallimard, 1989, p, 34). Qtd. in Bauman (1997).

Kroll, Jack. Review of True West. Dir. Joseph Papp. Public Theatre production. "California Dreaming". *Theatre* Jan 5, 1981.

Lesser, Wendy. Review of *True West*. Dir. Robert Woodruff. Magic Theatre Production, San Francisco, July / Sept. 1980. *The Three Penny Review*, Winter 1981.

Mc Kelley, James. "The Artist and the West". *Western American Literature* xxvi: 4 (1992).

Mottram, Ron. *Inner Landscape*. Columbia: University of Missouri Press, 1984.

Patraka, Vivien and M. Siegel. *Sam Shepard*. Boise, Idaho: Boise state University Printing & Graphic Services, 1985.

Rosen, Carol. "Emotional Territory :An Interview with Sam Shepard". *Modern Drama*, 36:1 (1993).

Sharett, Christopher, ed. *Crisis Cinema: The Apocalypse Idea in Postmodern Narrative Film*. Washington D.C Maisonneuve Press, 1993.

Shepard, Sam. *Angel City and Other Plays*. New York: Urizen Books, 1977.

_____. *Seduced. Fool for Love and Other Plays*. N.Y: Bantam Books, 1988.

_____. *True West, Seven Plays*, N.Y: Bantam Books, 1981.

_____. *Man Fly*. Qtd. in Patrick J. Fennet. Ibid.

_____. Qtd. in David Copelin. "From Theatre to Film and Back". (Sam Shepard and Stage director Robert Calhoun talks about *Angel City* to Taper Literary Manager David Copelin during the rehearsal of *Angel City*). n.d.

Wade, Leslie A. *Sam Shepard and the American Theatre*. Westport, Connecticut: Greenwood Press, 1997.

Wileox, Leonard. "West's The Day of Locust and Shepard's Angel City: Refiguring L.A. Noir". *Modern Drama*, 30:1 (1993).

Zinman, Toby Silverman. "Visual Histrionics: Shepard's Theatre of the *First Wall*". Reprinted by permission from *Theatre Journal*, December 1988, @John Hopkins University Press, 1988.

Conclusion

Sam Shepard is considered as one of the latest icons of American theatre who is often compared with other icons of American culture like Hemingway, Huck Finn, Audie Murphy, John Wayne. Even his individual image reflects a prototype of a typical American figure. On the book covers, photographs and film publicity materials, he mostly appears in western outfit with a cowboy hat. On the cover of his book, *Motel Chronicle* (1982), he appears in typical western costume with a coke bottle in his hand, standing beside a coach with Texas licence plate. In the picture he looks at the camera, but most of the times he would avoid looking at the camera as in the 2006 DVD cover of *Don't Come Knocking*. This diversion is suggestive of his "impractical rural modesty", writes Leslie Wade (143). He, writes Wade, "prefers to look towards the horizon and exude a frontier appeal that 'intimates a secretive understanding of his native soil" (143).

This is typical Sam Shepard, the 'rodeo rider' of American theatre. His personality reflects the open range of America's national imagination. And works his betray the intimate spontaneity of his own Americanness. His works are not part of a narrative body that uncritically celebrates national obsessions; rather they disturbingly betray the terror that lashes out at the collective consciousness of America, the nation. His plays, wrote John Lahr, "flush out the hidden yearnings and terrors of the American collective unconscious" (136).

The achievement of Shepard lies in giving the American preoccupation with cultural fear a dramatic expression, and this elemental preoccupation forms one of the important themes in his plays. He redraws the cultural cartography of America with intimate cultural signs. This intimacy is acquired not only through themes, it is achieved, as Ruby Cohn put it, through "images and rhythms" (185). Shepard draws his images and rhythms from the familiar sites of popular culture and mass media, which made him intensely contemporary and profoundly American. He has given legitimacy to the intimate cultural signs that preoccupy the American cultural mind. In his plays he has most effectively turned the figures of popular culture into lasting patterns of myths by assigning them new aesthetic meanings without dislodging their established semantic values as cultural symbols. Ruby Cohn points out, "like his ancestor O'Neil...Shepard in maturity is dramatising a tragic America, mired in sin like the Fitzgerald of *Great Gatsby*." According to her, "Shepard is at once seduced by and critical of American wealth and its artefacts. Like Thomas, he realises that 'you can't go home again' – to a pastoral civilisation" (Cohn, 185). Shepard reflects this awareness with an abiding intimacy.

The protagonists in Shepard look for the idioms to invent a new narrative which can assure a sense of freedom, personal integrity and wholeness. They strive to achieve the mental status to be able to live beyond their current identity which is primarily a constructed image that they voluntarily carry as their authentic persona. Henry Heckamore in *Seduced* (1978) metamorphosed into an image that is not destructible even by bullets. Henry becomes a victim of his own apotheosis.

Melodrama Play (1967) makes a significant beginning in Shepard's dramatic career as this was the first play where he used rock music as one of the integral theatrical tools. This is also his first dramatic endeavour to deal with the problematics associated with artist's role in a society where art is treated as a product like any other consumer durables. This theme of creativity and conflict in artists reappears in his later plays: *Mad Dog Blues (1971), Cowboy Mouth* (1971), *Tooth of Crime* (1972) and *Geography of a Horse Dreamer* (1974).

The protagonists in *Mad Dog Blues* and *Cowboy Mouth* along with *Back Bog Beast Bait* (produced at the American Place Theatre on 29 April, 1971, on the same programme with

Cowboy Mouth) reflect a deep sense of angst and compulsive obsession to escape from being immured in the ubiquitous prisons of cultural politics. The artists in Sam Shepard, smarting from the state of confusion, are engaged in a conflict of dual desperation of fear and material temptations. The issue of artist's conflict with the new order of production modalities continues to dominate the plays that followed the 'rock plays' of Shepard of the early seventies. *Tooth of Crime* exudes great power and makes a decisive impact upon the audience through its invention of a new language for theatre. In this play Shepard successfully merges context and language with each other and this was what had become the dominant dramatic force in the plays that followed – *Geography of a Horse Dreamer, Angel City, Suicide in B-flat.* The issue of corruption of artistic environment through commercial forces and the degeneration of artistic values receive mature treatment in his 1980 play, *True West.*

The confusion and the unease experienced by the artists can be understood in terms of Lyotardian paradigm of 'performativity'. The artist is poised against a setting of technological supremacy wherein originality is a secondary virtue. The scientific and technological advancement reduce any artistic creation into matters of manufacturing protocols of commercial industries, which demand "maximum output with minimum input". All the artists are forced to enter a system network wherein they are asked to deliver to their limits under duress. The artist is made into a pawn like Rabbit Brown in *Angel City* and Austin in *True West* who are enmeshed in technological games and their arts become absolutely subservient to the new cultural equations of "wealth, efficiency and truth". James Schevill, therefore, describes Shepard as a gifted playwright with a vision to reflect the confused, rapidly changing technological society along with the other grotesque changes (*Grotesque* 3). Shepard has also reflected the split between Jefferson's dream of an endless frontier land and Hamilton's vision of industrial centralisation. Against this backdrop of technological tyranny, the artist seeks a space of freedom through his pastoral nostalgia. He recalls his pastoral past with romantic fondness and rural naivety just as the way Niles in *Suicide* would recall his home in the island where the rain sounded like "Balinese cymbals on the roof" (*SBf* 211).

Shepard's artists belong to the Eisenhower romanticism of post-war America marking the time when the Hollywood dream machine continued to invent the images of a victorious America (the trend, however, continues till date), reflecting, as David J. DeRose would call, "a righteous and Audy Murphy America of heroic proportions and bigger than life stars and adventures" (2). He writes, "this was the time when the media generated myths grew to such proportions and with such speed that they lost all connection to the reality from where they once sprang" (2-3). Therefore, Schevil described Shepard's art heroes as "grotesque" (3). He called them so because the characters were part of American fantasies of power and fame, which, in paradoxically, fostered and distorted them. Henry Malcom Heckamore, the relic of his own fame and power in *Seduced*; the defeated Rock Star Hoss in *Tooth*; Rabbit, the degenerated actor in *Angel City* are all trapped in the imperial dream machine of American phantasmagoria. Shepard underlines the vacuity of such dreams through his subtle lampooning of the system that reproduces the dreams through the contours of various narratives. Hollywood is one such narrative that transforms the countryside innocence of Rabbit Brown into a sci-fi monstrosity.

The protagonists in Shepard are fragmented and desperate, devoid of coherence and totality. They are caught in a condition of ontological 'insecurity' having led a life without feeling 'alive' (Henry Heckamore desperately seeks to experience how it feels to live a life). Cody in *Geography* implores Santee to let him be in 'Great nature' which he had not seen for years. He has the fear that the sun might blind him for he had no experience of leading an existence by himself.

Shepard parades his artists against a backdrop which DeRose defined as 'unfixed'. The world of Shepard has abandoned the elements that used to ensure an individual's sense of wholeness, wherein they no longer can rediscover their own heritage, where the communal ritual of intimate social living is replaced by the multi-million dollar structures of lifestyle enclaves. Shepard's is a world, writes DeRose, "where man becomes a stranger all of a sudden and when he returns to the place that used to be his home becomes unrecognisable. This is also the world in which the 'artists have lost the roots of their inspiration and heroes don't remember what heroism is, the world that remains seemingly unchanged but that has actually turned into a foreign planet" (De Rose 5).

In its search for a form and content for articulation, the artistic obsession in Shepard has been to access a reachable memory. History becomes an unreliable site from where one can formulate a definition of the present, for the present turns out to be a gestalt of fragmented recollections of an assumed past and in the process the artist finds himself engaged amidst the exercise of reinventing the myths in retrospect. Niles in *Suicide* keeps on trying to define his identity through an assortment of images that he has been associated with. Henry in *Seduced* tries to outreach his own myth that was reconstructed by the fragments of his memory. Hoss in *Tooth* tries to arrogate his artistic identity by way of rediscovering the mythic image of his own, which, in effect, more a nostalgia than his private history. Art too, under such circumstances, becomes fragmented. Shepard writes in *Rolling Thunder Logbook*, "Art is a direct outcome of fractured memory" (1). It (art) becomes a reference to reassure oneself that "they sprang from somewhere" (*RTL* 45).

This pattern of reconstructing the past and aligning the myth with its physiognomy is a strategy at social survival what Johannes Birringer called, "a retrospective process". This process becomes a part of the artist's creative exercise through which he seeks an aesthtetic transformation of the social space in which he inhabits. He attempts a journey work through the historical trajectories to locate the lost sites of oblivion where he could once validate his authenticity. Kosmo in *Mad Dog Blues* resonates his urge for this transformation, "But I'm a musician! I've got to create. I've to get back to the city. Back to my lands. Back to my roots." (155)

Such a cultural scene makes it imperative to redefine the state of art and the status of the artist. This is where Sam Shepard becomes a profoundly significant cultural event, for his plays happen to have begun a new cultural debate by according a decisive legitimacy to a new generation of artist creators and their creations which accommodated in a secondary position in the cultural maps of modernist elites. Shepard provides a discoursal prestige to the art form that is a part of a were popular culture.

The artists, despite being part of a postmodern cultural landscape of America, are not gregarious insiders. They collectively form a destabilising force that strongly resist appropriation. They assert through paralogy—dissension—and categorically refuse to become an uncritical part, *vis a vis,* victims of the system. They do not settle for any consensus which could enable them to survive and flourish by being within the system. Consensus would subjugate them to manipulations. This awareness prompts the artists of Shepard to go to the extent of self obliteration as the final assertion of their power as creators.

The artists in Shepard frustrate the attempts of disciplining by the agencies of the power networks of culture through continual subversion of all such attempts. Despite being in the 'panopticon' of postmodern cultural order, the artists could register their formidable resistance of being disfigured. The crude attempts by the agencies of cultural corporations to discipline the artists in *Geography*, *Melodrama* or in *Cowboy* have conclusively failed. The artists in Shepard triumph as liberated entities albeit at times through self-destruction. They are postmodern not because they temporally belong to that cultural map, but because they also assert their paralogy in the true spirit of postmodern dissension.

Shepard, as a dramatist, discovers the myths that constitute the essence and the prehistory of the mass consciousness. He becomes a folklorist who captures in his warbling the images of common imaginations. Shepard is a people's man who disturbs the self complacency of material comfort by exposing the tragedy of cultural signs that the artists try to authenticate through the processes of their creative exercises. Shepard secures the confidence of his audience and readers because they could obtain a close cultural affinity with his universe. His universe is crowded like that of the world of Kosmo—haunted by Jimmy Hendrix, Janis Joplin, Buddy Holly, Big Bapper, Sar Cook, Jimmy Rogers, Brian James, Mae West or like the world of Austin and Lee (*True West*)—dominated by Kirk Douglas.

In Shepard's plays we come across the familiar icons: rock stars, Hollywood divas and matinee idols, jazz musicians and the like who form the cartography of America's cultural landscape. They constitute the class of America's new heroes and Shepard, as a visionary, manifests his ability to look at them beyond their apparent apotheotical realm. As an insider to the world of American heroism, he makes cultural documentation of their meteoric rise and their unceremonious fall. He records the moments of their victory and their defeat. He reveals a poignant cultural truth with oracular accuracy, "All the heroes is dying like flies, they say it's a sign a' the time." (*Tooth* 205)

Despite being, apparently, the biggest beneficiaries of the system in material terms, the artists, the stars, become ever more apprehensive of the system itself. They find themselves as the executioners of fatal deals. Shepard here celebrates the romanticism of tragic heroes who is ultimately afraid of the world, yet he longs to become a part of it:

> *Rabbit:* What is the most frightening thing in the world?
> *Tympani:* (Blankly) A space (he continues drums)
> *Rabbit:* What is the most frightening thing in the whole world?
> *Tympani:* A life cut off from all life.
>
> (*Angel City* 23)

The indomitable urge of the artist to return to the pastoral geography becomes a recurrent theme in the plays of Shepard. The protagonists make attempts to reach this elusive landscape by way of regenerating the ability to blur with the native space.

The act of writing drama has enabled Shepard to address the contesting forces within and outside, which he both identified and abandoned. The process of writing liberates him to establish a commune with himself at a more immediate level. Writing for him is both an experience of renewal and sublimation as drama for him is a metaphor for approximating the rediscovered intimacy with myriad form expressions. He informs, "I'm interested in exploring the writing of play through attitudes derived from other forms such as music, painting, sculpture, film etc." (qtd. in Foster 51). For him language is a veil that hides the demons and the angels that inhabit the characters, and their quest is for finding those forces hiding behind their own languages. For him this quest is to discover those forces, to have a showdown with them and bring an end to the mystery. This process of demystification involves death and rebirth. *Suicide in B-flat* essentially deals with this particular issue.

Shepard reveals: "The idea of dying and being reborn is really an interesting one. It's always there at the back of my head.... I was raised an Episcolian. But that was another kind of prison to get out of. You have this personality and somehow feel locked into it, jailed by all your cultural influences and your psychological ones from your family and all that." (Qtd. in Foster 51)

Shepard's urge for self renewal makes him impulsively aware of the possibility of another kind of world that is not confining like the one in which his artists are entrapped: "There is always that impulse that there is another kind of world, something that does not confine you that way...so what it means to die and be born again I've wanted somehow to get into." (Qtd. in Foster 51)

This has been the declared mission of Shepard to locate the 'other world', which is liberating and which one can only reach through rituals of renewal.

Shepard is a writer of intuitions and impulses. The arguments in the plays also take place at an intuitive level. Rick Foster makes a contrast of Shepard with Ibsen—a theatre architect that disciplined the materials of stagecraft and plot structures. Shepard's, on the other hand, are the works that have brilliantly improvised music within their structures. The word 'rift' is often applied to monologues. That is, when Ibsen's root metaphor is spatial, Shepard's is temporal. The progression in Shepard's plays is along the line from moment to moment. The text of *Tooth* forms one of the most successful discourses in typically Shepardian pattern of narrative.

The moment in Shepard's plays is important as they capture the theatrical fantasies of the author and his characters. For Shepard a fantasy is an important means for establishing a communion of understanding. He, in fact, exhorts his implied audience to share his fantasies in good faith.

Shepard informs: "If someone shares a fantasy with me, there is an understanding between us. However, the understanding may come to a painful end when the actual world is encountered and the two fantasists have radically different interpretations of the consequences of sharing. In the early stages of love affair the most shattering kind of arguments came from just this kind of understanding without understanding. Communist, Nazi, a Zionist, a Catholic and a businessman can sit in the same concert hall and the have the same 'understanding' of a symphony." (qtd. In Foster 53) Shepard's plays, therefore, tend to, as Foster points out, "move from fantasy to fantasy as operas move from aria to aria" (53).

Artist's conflict has been a familiar aspect for both radical and conservative critical schools. Conflict indicates, as is put by Christopher Sharett, "a sense of renewal". It suggests a cyclical "occurrence" that signals the necessity for an alternative set up for the Marxists and the re-establishment of the conventional and the existing institutions for the conservatives (for the capitalists interpret crisis as an aberration). In the postmodern culture, however, both 'crisis' and 'catastrophe' are interpreted as an epistemological as well as historical break that problematises the ontology of being. In the plays of Shepard the material condition, as in any postmodern society, constructs the dramatic world as a "crisis scene".

The artists in Shepard are trapped in a zone of conflict because any allegiance on their part to any one of the responses to overcome their crisis would further endanger their freedom.

The radical as well as the conservative responses to crisis are directed towards evolving and re-legitimising 'metanarratives'. The tenacity of their cultural vision seems to have led to their resolute resistance to the appropriating advances of the discourse in force in order to ensure untutored manifestation of their creative self. Therefore, Slim refuses to pose as a rock 'n' roll saviour in *Cowboy Mouth*; Cody denies to dream a scripted dream as was asked by his captors in *Geography*; Niles decides to disappear to pre-empt attempts of colonising his art by the intruders in *Suicide.*

The second band song in *Melodrama Play* subtly reveals the tragic irony that entails the subjective position of the artist in the society he lives in:

> Well now that you're older than ya' was before
> And ya' can tell that you are older
> 'Cause everything is a bore
> well now that you're clumsy instead of so quick
> ....
> 'Cause we're sunk on the ground
> And your heart even don't pound
> While you lay on the floor
> And they just ask you for more
> Of the same that ya gave
> Of the same that they took (131)

Cody in *Geography* asserts his autonomy and freedom by subverting attempts of being disciplined by his kidnapers. Cody, the dreamer, outrightly rejects to dream anything. He expresses his freedom despite being a hostage. He declares, to the perplexity of his captors, "I've got no worries, no troubles to work out. Everything is hunky dory" (*GHD* 92).

The resistance of the artists against the totalising cultural edifices is not taken up through agonised responses and self oppressive disciplining, which bewilder the opposing forces turning them clueless about their moves and actions. These forces are comfortable to take on the situations which can be described and explained in terms of their own idioms. Besides, by being 'disorderly' in their strategies to resist the determining forces, the artists pre-empt the possibility of falling in the trap of the discourses of those forces. Their elusive and incoherent resistance as well as their cryptic passivity shake and threaten the establishment. The artist is never ostensibly challenges the violence of his surroundings; he is rather disturbingly passive and torturously receptive of the atrocities inflicted upon him. Physically he is weak. But he is disruptive through his creative expressions. His subtle resistance and his compulsive subversion of all logical predications push the subjugating forces of the society to the brink of insanity. As for Pablo and Louis in *Suicide*, their encounter with the world of Niles is an experience of insanity where "everything is crazy" and where they are vulnerably exposed to the danger of going 'mad'.

The artists in Shepard pose a serious threat to the onward horizontality of the cultural march. Shepard's artists are like the Foucauldian figures who represent the disjunctive vertical identities in the horizontal architecture of cultural rubrics. They affect the disruption, through madness (Henry Hecakmore, Niles, Cody) or through death (Hoss, Niles) whereby the tyranny of reason of the governing order is effectively thwarted. The vertical posture of the artist is a means to retreat into the realms of aesthetic liberation or fractal freedom atomising a motion against totalisation.

Ihab Hassan's concept of "Radical Innocence" (the term he borrowed from Yeats's "Prayer for My Daughter") can explain the innocent pride of Shepard's artists in refusing to accept 'reality's rules'. Sheapard presents a case of confrontation between the innocence of the artist and the destructive reality of experience. The confrontation reaches the high point of crisis when the reality turns out to be an experience that is related to the discovery of limits within the narrow world of conventional specificities. The artist encounters crisis even when the privacy of dreams is regulated. Cody in G*eography* complains that the ideal environment is not there for him to dream because he needs a "better situation" where the "windows" should not be "blocked" (*GHD* 283).

Ihab Hassan in his autobiography, *Out of Egypt* (1986), asked the question, "Can (man) learn to dream again and, dreaming wake, to mediate actively between Culture and Desire, Language and Power, History and Hope?" (15). Shepard seems to have similar anxieties. Culturally his hero is a decentered entity. He is, as he himself describes, "fragmented bits of pieces", "unorganised". He undergoes several phases of crisis in various forms that threaten to the extent of physically destroying them. As in *Seduced* Henry Heckamore is compelled to go in self exile; while Niles in *Suicide* is forced to attempt self obliteration; Hoss in *Tooth* is left with no other option but to commit suicide; Rabbit Brown in *Angel City* compulsively degenerates into a slimy creature while Austin in *True West* decides to vanish in the vast horizon of the Western desert. They exit from the social space primarily because their societal history fails to assure any salvation for them. Here there is "nothing real" ("There's nothing real down here", says Austin in *True West,* 49), everything is fake, everybody is with a mask ("I believe in my mask" sings Crow in *Tooth* 235).

The artist is exposed to repressive power relations wherein his very existence is imperilled. He is subjected to physical subjugation by the imperialist forces of culture corporations. The process of subjugation is obvious in the plays like *Melodrama Play*, *Cowboy Mouth, Geography of a Horse Dreamer* where the artist is imprisoned inside a prototype of Foucauldian panopticon. This incarceration of artist is more subtle and pervasive in the plays like *Suicide in B-flat, Angel City, True West,* and *Mad Dog Blues.* In these plays the self incarceration of artists is necessitated following the hazardous coercion of the forces of the outside world that potentially threaten them to destroy. Henry, therefore, frantically instructs Raul to lower the curtains because "Anything could be out there tryin' to get in" (*Seduced* 254). Niles in *Suicide* is an artist by birth whose own voice shocked him to a emotional awareness as he finds himself with an imperilled body lacerated by the brutal forces of the outside world. Hence, he makes a virtual exit form this world because "It's a trap! It's worse than a trap!" (*SB-f* 228).

The outside world either tries to colonise artistic gift of the creator or makes attempt to destroy his artistic ability with the intention to rob the artist of the very source of his power. The incarcerated creator is confined in enclosures that are shut out to the space outside. The artist is not allowed to have any access to the reality that lies beyond the confines of the 'panoptican'. Duke, Slim, Cody all look for an access to the world outside their claustrophobic confinements—their native mainstay. They are transported to a location which is not their own. They are thrown into an alien geography where their confident creative freedom collapses and makes him powerless. The abductors make earnest attempts to enslave the artist by regulating his conceits (*True West, Melodrama Play*); the contours of his imagination (*Angel City*); his palpable voice (*Suicide, Tooth*) and the privacy of his dreams (*Geography*).

Inside the fortified confinement the artists is reduced into a powerless figurehead devoid of his freedom. The imploring seer can no longer impulsively create and dream as manifestations of his creative liberation. In his book, *Radical Innocence*, Ihab Hassan almost prophetically proclaims:

> Men seem to know by instinct that dreams are monstrous things that should never see the light of day. Men tempt the hero to realise their dreams, and then punish him for his daring credulousness. In a limited sense, therefore, every hero is a scapegoat, and a radical innocent. Thus was Prometheus chained to rock and Oedipus banished from Thebes. Thus too in a more subtle fashion was Faust self damned and Christ crucified. (326-327)

Shepard's heroes are cultural abstractions; they are the allegories of contemporary cultural symbols. The issue of locating an authentic and intimate cultural space continues to dominate the theme of these plays. The hero's source of creative knowledge is cut off and he is emasculated. The situation justifies an analogy with Foucauldian paradigm where knowledge and power are hyphenated complimentaries to each other. Knowledge extends and reinforces power and power produces knowledge. By way of disrupting this dynamics the artist is reduced into a veritable cultural subaltern as in Shepard's plays the subjugation is not mere psychological or political. The process of disempowering the artist is carried out through physical atrocities and imploring violence of cultural terrorism as well. In *Geography* Cody is tied to the foot of a bed and is forced to lie as a "crucified artist" and is subjected to constant mauling by the corporate agents.

Shepard's protagonists wage a fight to escape from what Jim Collins would call "circle of reality". The artist is engaged in the struggle of liberating himself from the determining structures of their imposed identities. There is an obvert tension of the subject in his compulsion to represent his socially given identity and his perpetual struggle to relocate the private autonomy of his existence. The artist protagonist in Shepard confronts an acute crisis as they resist to be reduced into what the socially given identities force them to become. At the same time they are yet to attain the autonomy to relocate a space for themselves outside the world of ordering forces.

The consequences that they often end up with turn them into tragic heroes who are exposed to the finality of the absence of a cultural order conducive for creative freedom. They are forced to exit the social space, like Travis in *Paris, Texas*, while in search for an imagined destiny.

The anthropological explanation of Cliford Geertz informs us that man, like ideas, values, emotions, and even nervous system, is a product of a given culture whose self is fashioned according to the generative rules of the given cultural order. He explains that man's individuality is guided by the cultural patterns, as well as the historically created systems of meaning which determine form, order, point of view and direction (5-9). As culture shapes man into single species so does it shapes man as separate individual who defies even the powerful establishment of a cross-cultural consensus. He defies with 'paralogy'. Shepard deals with the individuals, who despite being a part of a common system of signification, differ from the general body of the community. Against uncritical resignation to his lot, Shepard's heroes assert dissension by challenging the normative codes of institutional culture.

Neil Carson characterises tragic hero as :

> All the tragic heroes from Orestes to Macbeth, we are told, are destroyed in attempting to obtain their rightful place in society. What distinguishes the tragic from the mass of ordinary man in his willingness to *question* and *attack* the scheme of things that degrade him. (80 *italics* mine)

In Shepard the hero does not fight an individual enemy, he takes on the system that attempts to make him part of the totalitarian hegemony. He adopts the strategy to fragment and disintegrates his own self in order to elude categorisation.

The hero in Shepard attempts to construct new boundaries of assertion by breaking the impregnable fortress of "civilised culture". They strive toward locating a homeland at the edge of 'civilisation' with a powerful optimistic note to "rocking Bethlehem to be born" to find what Shepard calls "a new innocence".

Works Cited

Althusser, Louis. "Ideology and Ideological State Apparatus". *Lenin and Philosophy and Other Essays*. Tr. Bren Brewster. London: New left Books, 1971.

Birringer, Johannes. *Theatre, Theory, Postmedernism*. Bloomington, Indianapolis: Indiana University Press, 1991.

Carson, Neil. *Arthur Miller*. London: Macmillan, 1982.

Cohn, Ruby. *New American Dramatists: 1960-1980*. New York: Groove Press Inc., 1982.

Collins, Jim. *Uncommon Culture: Popular Culture and Postmodernism*. NewYork: Routledge.

DeRose, David. *Sam Shepard*. New York: Tawane Publishers, 1982.

Foster, Rick. "The Genius Sam Shepard: Art is made out of arguments with ourselves". n.d. p.5

Geertz, Clifford. "The Impact of the Concept f Culture on the Concept of Man". *The Interpretation of Cultures: Selected Essays*. New York: Basic Books, 1971. (included in *New Historicism and Cultural Materialism*. Ed. Kiernan Ryan. London: Arnold, 1996).

Hassan, Ihab. *Radical Innocence*. Princeton, New Jersey: Princeton University Press, 1961.

Lahr, John. "Playing Fast and Loose", *TLS*, 24 November 1975.

Lyotard, Jean Francois. *The Postmodern Conditions: A Report on Knowledge*. Tr. Geoff Benington and Brian Masumi. Manchester: Manchester University Press, 1984.

Mottram, Ron. *Inner Landscape*. Columbia: University of Missouri Press, 1984.

Scevill, James. "American Grotesque: Sam Shepard's *Buried Child*". *1979-80 Humanities Dramatic Work as a Cultural/ Historical/ Document*. Rhodes Island Committee for Humanities.

Shepard, Sam. *Rolling Thunder Logbook.* New York: Limelight Edition, 1987.

_____ . *Mad Dog Blues and Other Plays.* (includes *The Rock Garden, Cowboys No. 2, Cowboy Mouth, Blue Bitch* and *Nightwalk).* New York: Winter House, 1972.

_____. *Seven Plays.* (includes *Buried Child, Tooth of Crime, La Turista, True West, Tongues,* and *Savage Love*). New York: Bantam Books, 1981.

_____. *Angel City and Other Plays.* New York: Urizen Books, 1977

Sheridan, Alan. *Michel Foucault: The Will to Truth.* London: Travistock Publications, 1982.

Wade, Leslie A. *Sam Shepard and the American Theatre. Westwood*: Greenwood Press, 1997.

Bibliography

Primary Sources

Shepard, Sam. *Rolling Thunder Logbook.* New York: Limelight Edition, 1987.

_____. *Five Plays by Sam Shepard: Chicago, Icarus's Mother, Red Cross, Fourteen Hundred Thousand, Melodrama Play*. Indianapolis: Bobbs-Merrill, 1967.

_____. *Mad Dog Blues and Other Plays.* (includes *The Rock Garden, Cowboys No. 2, Cowboy Mouth, Blue Bitch* and *Nightwalk).* New York: Winter House, 1972.

_____. *Seven Plays.* (includes *Buried Child, Tooth of Crime, La Turista, True West, Tongues,* and *Savage / Love*). New York: Bantam Books, 1981

_____. *Angel City and Other Plays*. New York: Urizen Books, 1977.

_____. *Seduced. Fool for Love and Other Plays*. N.Y: Bantam Books, 1988.

_____. *Cowboy Mouth*. Food For Love and Other Plays (1984).

_____. *The Mad Dog Blues and Other Plays* (1972).

_____. *Melodrama Play, Angel City and Other Plays* (1977).

_____. *Geography of a Horse Dreamer*. London: Faber and Faber, 1977.

_____. *Man Fly*. Qtd. in Patrick J. Fennet. Ibid.

_____. *Suicide in B.Flat. Angel City and Other Plays*. New York: Urizen Books, 1977.

_____. *Angel City and Other Plays..* New York: Urizen Books, 1977.

_____. *Geography of a Horse Dreamer, Suicide in B-flat, Seduced, Fool for Love and other Plays.* New York: Bantam Books, 1984.

_____. *The Mirror of Production.* Trans. Mark Poster. St. Louis: Telos Press, 1975.

_____. *The Unseen Hand and Other Plays*. (Contains: *The Unseen Hand, Forensic & the Navigators, The Holy Ghostly, Back Bog Beast Bait, Shaved Splits, 4-H Club*). New York: Vintage Books, 1996.

_____. *Action and The Unseen Hand: Two Plays*. London: Faber and Faber, 1975

_____. *Angel City & Other Plays*. (Contains: Gelber, "SAM SHEPARD: The Playwright as Shaman," Angel *City*, *Curse of the Starving Class*, *Killer's Head*, *Action*, *Mad Dog Blues*, *Cowboy Mouth*, *The Rock Garden*, *Cowboys #2* "Sam Shepard: 9 Random Years [7 + 2]" by Patti Smith. New York: Applause Theatre Book Publishers, 976.

_____. *Mad Dog Blues & Other Plays*. (The Winter Repertory, v.4). Contains: *Mad Dog Blues*, *Cowboy Mouth*, *The Rock Garden*, *Cowboys #2*, *Blue Bitch*, *Nightwalk*. *New* York: Winter House, 1972.

_____. *Chicago and Other Plays*. New York: Applause Theatre Book Publishers, 1981.

_____. *The Unseen Hand and Other Plays*. (Contains: *The Unseen Hand*, *Rock Garden*, *Chicago*, *Icarus's Mothe*, *4-H Club*, *Fourteen Hundred Thousand*, *Red Cross*, *Cowboys No. 2*, *Forensic and the Navigators*, *The Holy Ghostly*, *Operation Sidewinder*, *Mad Dog Blues*, *Back Bog Beast Bait*, *Killer's Head)*. *New* York: Bantam Books, 1986.

_____. *Curse of the Starving Class: A Play in Three Acts*. New York: Dramatists Play Service, 1976.

__. *The Late Henry Moss, Eyes for Consuela, When the World Was Green:. Three Plays*. New York: Vintage, 1998.

_____. *States of Shock, Far North, Silent Tongue*. *New* York: Vintage Books, 1993.

_____. *The Unseen Hand and Other Plays*. (Contains: *The Unseen Hand*, *Forensic & the Navigators*, *The Holy Ghostly*, *Back Bog Beast Bait*, *Shaved Splits*, *4-H Club*). Indianapolis: Bobbs-Merrill, 1971.

_____. *The Holy Ghostly*. *In Best Short Plays of the World Theatre, 1968-1973* Ed. with an introduction and prefaces to the plays, Standley Richards. New York: Crown, 1973.

_____. *The Late Henry Moss, Eyes for Consuela, When the World Was Green: Three Plays*. New York: Vintage, 1998.

_____. *A Lie of the Mind and The War in Heaven: Angel's Monologue*. New York: New American Library, 1987.

_____. *A lie of the mind: a play in three acts*. San Francisco, CA: Union Press; 1993.

_____. *Maxagasm: A Distorted Western for Soul & Psyche*. 2nd drft. Los Angeles: Creative Management Associates, 1970.

_____. *Fool for Love and Other Plays* (Contains: *Fool for Love*; *Angel City*; *Melodrama Play*; with Patti Smith, *Cowboy Mouth*; *Action*; *Suicide in B Flat*; *Seduced*; *Geography of a Horse Dreamer*). Toronto and New York: Bantam, 1984.

_____. *Nightwalk* and *Terminal*. With Jean-Claude van Itallie, Megan Terry and the Open Theater. *Three Works by the Open Theater*. Ed. Karen Malpede. New York: Drama Book Specialists, 1974.

_____. *Paris, Texas*. New York : [Los Angeles] Gray City, Inc.; [Script Collectors Service], 1983 Hollywood: Script City, 1983. Screenplay. Berlin: Road Movies, 1984.

_____. *Operation Sidewinder: A Play in Two Acts.* In *Esquire*, 71 (May 1969).

_____. *Red Cross.* in *The New Underground Theater.* Ed. by Robert Schroeder. New York: Bantam Books, 1974.

_____. *The Rock Garden (Scene 3).* In *Oh! Calcutta! An Entertainment with Music.* By Kenneth Tynan. New York: Grove, 1969.

_____. *The Sad Lament of Pecos Bill on the Eve of Killing His Wife.* In *Theatre*, 12 (Summer/Fall 1981), pp. 32-38.

_____. *Sam Shepard: Seven Plays.* (Contains: *True West*; *Buried Child*; *Curse of the Starving Class*; *The Tooth of Crime (A Play with Music in Two Acts)*; *La Turista*; with Joseph Chaikin, *Tongues* (A Piece for Voice and Percussion) and *Savage/Love*). Intro. Richard Gilman. New York and Toronto: Bantam, 1981.

_____. *Seduced: A Play in Two Acts.* New York: Dramatists Play Service, 1979.

_____. *Shaved Splits.* In *Screw* magazine, 21 June 1971, pp. 3-7, 16.

_____. *Simpatico.* New York: Dramatists Play Service, 1995.

_____. *States of Shock, Far North, Silent Tongue.* New York: Vintage Books, 1993

_____. "Excerpts from Slave of the Camera," *Antaeus*, 66 (Spring 1991), pp. 421-429.

_____. *States of Shock.* in *Ten Screen Plays.* (Includes: *States of Shock, A Vaudeville Nightmare*, *Far North*, and *Silent Tongue*). New York: Vintage, 1993.

_____. *Suicide in B Flat: A Mysterious Overture.* New York: Lois Berman, 1978.

_____. *The War in Heaven (Aagel's Monologue).* Cowriter Joseph Chaikin. *Performing Arts Journal '85*, 9, pp. 249-62.

_____. *The Late Henry Moss, Eyes for Consuela, When the World Was Green: Three Plays.* New York: Vintage, 1998.

_____. *Zabriskie Point.* New York: Simon and Schuster, 1972.

Newspapers and Magazines

_____. "American Experimental Theatre Then and Now," *Performing Arts Journal*, 2 (Fall 1977), pp. 13-24 (Shepard, pp. 13-14). Reprinted in Marranca, ed., *American Dreams.* Performing Arts Journal, 1981, pp. 212-213.

_____. "Autobiography," *News of the American Place Theatre*, 3 (April 1971).

_____. "Language, Visualization, and the Inner Library," *Drama Review*, 21:4 (Dec 1977).

_____. "Less Than Half a Minute," *Time Out*, (July 12-18, 1974), pp. 16-17.

_____. "Metaphors, Mad Dogs and Old-Time Cowboys," *Theatre Quarterly*, 4 (Aug-Oct 1974), pp. 3-16.

_____. "News Blues," *Time Out*, 222 (May 31-June 6, 1974), p. 17.

_____. "OOB and the Playwright: Two Commentaries," *Works*, 1 (Winter 1968), pp.70-73. Tom Sankly, cowriter.

_____. "Sam Shepard, Playwright," *Performing Arts Journal,* 26 (Fall 1977), pp. 13-24.

_____. "Symposium: Playwrighting in America," *Yale/Theatre*, 4 (Winter 1973), pp. 8-27.

_____."Time," *Theatre*, 9 (Spring, 1978), p. 9. Appeared earlier in the *American Place Theatre Newsletter*, 1975. Reprinted in Marranca, ed., *American Dreams*.

_____. "True Dylan," *Esquire*, 108.1 (Jul 1987), pp. 59-68.

_____. "Visualization, Language and The Inner Library," *Drama Review*, 21 (December 1977), pp. 49-58. Reprinted in Marranca, ed., *American Dreams*.

Prose and Poetry

_____.*Cruising Paradise, Tales*. New York: Vintage Books, 1997.

_____. *Hawk Moon: A Book of Short Stories, Poems, and Monologues*. New York: Performing Arts Journal Publications, 1981

_____. *Motel Chronicles and Hawk Moon.* London: Faber and Faber, 1985.

_____. *Rolling Thunder Logbook.* New York: Limelight Editions, 1987

Unpublished Works of Sam Shepard

1. *Dog*
2. *Up to Thursday*
3. *Inacoma*
4. *Jacaranda*
5. *Little Ocean*
6. *Rocking Chair*

Secondary Sources

Aissis, Arline. Review of Seduced. Dit. Adrian Hall, Trinity Square Reportory Co., "Providence. Surrealistic Theatre is seducing". (Prof. Jasbin Jain's News Clipping File). n.p.

Althusser, Louis. "Ideology and Ideological State Apparatus". *Lenin and Philosophy and Other Essays*. Tr. Bren Brewster. London: New left Books, 1971.

Banes, Sally. *Greenwich Vilage*. Durham NC: Duke University Press, 1993.

Berman, Paul. "Shepardsets." *Nation*. 1984 Dec 29; 724.

Bigelow, Ernest Alanson, Jr. "A Symposium of Voices: Sam Shepard's Theater (Shepard Sam, Alter Egos, Monologue, Role Reversal)." *Dissertation Abstracts International* (53/03) 665; Ph.D.: State University of New York at Buffalo; 1992.

Burk, Robert Eugene, Jr. "Reading Shepard and Lacan: A Dramaturgy of the Subject." *Dissertation Abstracts International* (47/12) 4326; Ph.D.: University of Washington; 1986.

Baudrillard, Jean. *Selected Writings*. Ed. Mark Poster. Cambridge: Polity Press, 1988.

Baudrilliard, Jean. "The Ecstasy of Communication". Trans. John Johnston. *The Anti-Aesthetic*. Ed. Hall Foster. Port Townsend. Washington: Bay Press, 1983.

Bauman, Zygmunt. *Postmodernity and Its Discontent.* New York: New York UP, 1997.

Benet, Carol. *Sam Shepard on the German Stage: Critics, Politics, Myths.* New York, Frankfurt am Main: Peter Lang Publishing Inc., 1993.

Bigsby, C.W.E. *Modern American Drama: 1945-1990.* Cambridge: Cambridge UP, 1992.

Birringer, Johannes. *Theatre, Theory, Postmodernism.* Indianapolis: Indianapolis University Press, 1991.

Bottoms, Stephen J. *The Theatre of Sam Shepard: States of Crisis (Cambridge Studies in American Theatre and Drama)* Cambridge: Cambridge UP, 1998

Carson, Neil. *Arthur Miller*. London: Macmillan, 1982.

Chaikin, Joseph. *The War in Heaven*. New York: Blank Tape Studios; 1985.

Chubb, Kenneth. "Metaphors, Mad Dogs and Old Time Cow Boys: An Interview with Sam Shepard". Ed. Bonnie Maranca, *American Dream: The Imagination of Sam Shepard.* New York: Performing Arts Journal Publications, 1981.

Cima, Gay Gibson. "Shifting Perspectives: Combining Shepard and Rauschenberg." *Theatre Journal*. 1986 Mar; (1): 67-81.

Coe, Robert. "Image Ghosts are Blown." *The Rock Plays*. Bonnie Maranca. Ed. (1981).

Cohn, Ruby. *New American Dramatists: 1960-1980*. New York: Groove Press Inc., 1982

Collins, Jim. *Uncommon Culture*: *Popular Culture and Postmodernism.* NewYork: Routledge, 1989.

Comolli, Jean Luc and Jean Narboni. "Cinema, Ideology, Criticism". *Movies and Methods*, Vol. I. Ed. Bill Nichols. California: Berkley University of California Press, 1976.

Copelin, David. Interview. "From Theatre to Film and Back". Interview of Sam Shepard and Robert Calhoun, *Taper Literature Magazine* (n.d.) D-H.

Cott, Jonathan. Qtd. ı Patrick J. Fennel. "Shepard's Lost Sheep." *Sam Shepard: A Case Book*. Ed. King Kimball. NY: Garland, 1988.

_____. "The Rolling Stone Interview—Sam Shepard." *Rolling Stone*. 1986 Dec 18; (489-490): 166-172, 198, 200.

Davies, Mike. "City of Quartz: Excavating the Future in L.A." New York: 1990. (qtd. in)

De Rose, David J. *Sam Shepard*. New York: Tawane Publishers, 1982.

Downey, Robert. "Inside the Words". *Time Out*, April, 1977.

Dylan, Bob. *Knocked out Loaded*. Secaucus, N.J.: Warner Bros. Publications; 1986.

Ellington, Duke, Interview. "SABATA'S JAZZ: AN ARGENTINIAN ARTIST LOOKS AT AMERICA'S MUSIC". Geoffrey C. Ward. *American Heritage*, October, 1995.

Feigngold, Michael. *Grove New American Theatre*. New York: Grove Press, 1993.

Feingold, Michael. "Kleist and Shepard Flirt with Death", *The Village VOICE*, November 15, 1976.

Fennell, Patrick J. "Angel City." *Educational Theatre Journal*. 1977 Mar; 112-13.

Firth, Simon, *Sound Effect: Youth Leisure and the Politics of Rock 'n' Roll*. New York; Pantheon, 1981.

Freedman, Morris. American Drama in School Context. Carbondale, Southern Illinois UP, 1971.

Foster, Rick. "Sam Shepard: Art is made out of argument with ourselves." n.d.

Foster, Rick. "The Genius Sam Shepard: Art is made out of arguments with ourselves". n.d. p.5

Foucault, Michel. "Nietzche, Geneology, History". *Language, Counter Memory, Practice: Selected Essays and Interview*. Eds & trs. D.F. Bounchard and S. Simon. Oxford: Blackwell, 1977.

Gilaman, Richard. *Sam Shepard: Seven Plays*. New York: Bantam Books, 1981.

Geertz, Clifford. "The Impact of the Concept of Culture on the Concept of Man". *The Interpretation of Cultures: Selected Essays*. New York: Basic Books, 1971. (included in *New Historicism and Cultural Materialism*. Ed. Kiernan Ryan. London: Arnold, 1996)

Goldberg, Robert. "Off Off Broadway's Street Cowboy". *Rolling Stone's College Paper*, October, 1994.

Goldberg, Robert. "Sam Shepard: Off Broadway's Street Cowboy." *Rolling Stone College Paper* Oct. 1980.

Foucault, Michel. "Nietzche, Geneology, History". *Language, Counter Memory, Practice: Selected Essays and Interview*. Eds & trs. D.F. Bounchard and S.Simon. Oxford: Blackwell, 1977.

Goldman, Lucien. "The Genetic Structuralist Method in the History of Literature." *Towards a Sociology of the Novel*. Tr. Alan Sheridan. London: Tavistock, 1975.

Gregory, Lanier W. "The Killer's Ancvient Mask: Unity and Dualism in Shepard's *Tooth of Crime*". Toronto: *Modern Drama*, 36:1 (1993).

Gilman, Richard. "Introduction". *Sam Shepard: Seven Plays*. New York: Bantam Books, 1981.

Hall, Ann C. "Fire in the Snow: Shepard's Female Saviors." *Theatre Criticism*. Ed. Stanley Kauffman. New York: Performing Arts Journal Publications, 1983.

Hall, Ann C. "Fire in the Snow Shepard's Female Saviors." *A Kind of Alaska: Women in the Plays of O'Neil, Pinter and Shepard*. Carbondale: Southern Illinois UP, 1993.

Hassan, Ihab. *Radical Innocence*. Princeton, New Jersey: Princeton University Press, 1961

Hayes, Michael J. "Sam Shepard". *American Drama*. Ed. Clive Bloom. Kentucky: Macmillan, 1995.

Heyman, Ronlad. *Theatre and Anti-Theatre: Movements since Beckett*. New York: Oxford UP, 1979.

Hart, Lynda. *Sam Shepard's Metaphoric Stages*. New York, London: Green Press, 1987.

Hoeper, Jeffrey D. "Cain, Canaanites and Philistines in Sam Shepard's True West", Modern Drama 36:1 (1993).

Haber, Fern. *Beyond Postmodern Politics: Lyotard, Rorty, Foucault*. New York: Routledge, 1994.

Hart, Lynda. "Sam Shepard's Pornographic Visions" *Studies in Literary Imagination*. 21: 2 (1988).

Herman William. *Understanding American Drama*. Carolina: University of South Carolina Press, 1987.

Jabes, Edmund. "Un etranger avee, saus le bras, un livre du petiti format" (Paris: Gallimard, 1989, p, 34). Qtd. in Bauman (1997).

Jain, Jasbir. "The West and the Plays of Sam Shepard". *Literature and Popular Culture: A Festschrift for Isaac Sequira*. Eds. R.S. Sharma, Sukhbir Singh *et al. Hyderabad*: Cauvery Publications, 1983.

Jameson, Frederick. "Postmodernism and Consumer Society". *The Anti-Aesthetic: Essays on Postmodern Culture*. Ed. Hall Foster. Port Townsend, 1983.

Kroll, Jack, constantee Guthrie and Janet Huck. "Who is that tall, dark stranger?" *Newsweek*, 11 November, 1985.

Kroll, Jack. Review of True West. Dir. Joseph Papp. Public Theatre production. "California Dreaming". Theatre Jan 5, 1981.

Lechte, John. "Theodor Adorno". *Fifty Key Contemporary Thinkers: From Structuralism to Postmodernity*., London: Routledge, 1996.

_____. "Maurice Blonchet." (1996).

Lesser, Wendy. "Review of True West". Dir. Robert Woodruff. Magic Theatre Production, San Francisco, July / Sept. 1980. The Three Penny Review, Winter 1981.

Lahr, John. "Playing Fast and Loose", *TLS,* 24 November 1975

Lyotard, Jean Francois. *The Postmodern Conditions: A Report on Knowledge.* Tr. Geoff Benington and Brian Masumi. Manchester: Manchester University Press, 1984

Malkin, Jeanctte P. Verbal *Violence in Contemporary Drama: From Handke to Shepard.* Cambridge, New York: Cambridge University Press, 1992.

Marsalis, Wynton. Interview. "What is Jazz". Tony Scherman. Reprinted by Permission from *American Heritage*, October 1995. © Forbes Inc. 1995.

Murch, Anne. "Genet-Triana-Kopit: Ritual as 'Danse Macabre'." *Modern Drama.* 1973 Mar; 369-81.

Mc Kelley, James. "The Artist and the West". Western American Literature xxvi: 4 (1992).

McBride, Stuart. "Sam Shepard-Listener and Playwright". Christian Science Monitor, 23 December, 1980.

McBride, Steward Dill. "Sam Shepard." *Christian Science Monitor.* 1980 Dec 23: 2-3 (1).

Mottram, Ron. *Inner Landscape.* Columbia: University of Missouri Press, 1984.

Moynihan, D. S. "Visual Music: CEMENT's Shepard Sets." *The Drama Review.* 1985 Jun; : 110-12.

Oumano, Ellen. *Sam Shepard: The Life and Work of American Dreamer.* New York: St. Martin's Press, 1986.

Pareles, Jon. "Music to Match the Beat in Early Shepard." *New York Times.* 1984 Nov 18: H4 (1).

Patraka, Vivien and M. Siegel. Sam Shepard. Boise, Idaho: Boise state University Printing & Graphic Services, 1985.

Protor, Elizabeth. "Off Beat Humours & Comic Mystery in Shepard's Plays." *La Turista*, The Unseen Hand, *"The Dog Blues and The Forensic and the Ñavigators."* Sam Shepard: A Case Book. Ed. King Kimball. NY: Garland Publishing Inc., 1988.

Poland, Albert and Bruce Mailman. Íntroduction". *The Off Off Broadway Book: The Plays, People, Theatre.* Indianapolis: The Bobb's Merill Co., 1972.

Patraka, Vivien M. & Mark Siegel. *Sam Shepard.* Boise State University, Boise Idaho, 1985.

Ponechen, Joseph. Review. "Yale Strikes Right Chord with Suicide in B-Flat". *Trumbull Times*, 1976.

Powe, Bruce. "Shepard's Way With Music". Toronto: *Modern Drama*, 36:1 (1993).

Powe, Bruce W. "The Tooth of Crime: Sam Shepard's Way with Music." *Modern Drama*. 1981 Mar; (1): 13-25, 39-46.

_____. "The Tooth of Crime: Sam Shepard's Way with Music."

Parker, Dorothy. *Essays on Modern American Drama.* Toronto: University of Toronto Press; 1987: 174-187.

Proctor, Elizabeth Clifton. "The Art of Sam Shepard (Modern Drama)." *Dissertation Abstracts International* (47/01) 181; Ph.D.: The University of North Carolina at Chapel Hill; 1985.

Red Clay Ramblers. *A Lie of the Mind.* Durham, N.C.: Sugar Hill Records; 1986; p1986.

Red Clay Ramblers. *A Lie of the Mind.* Salem, MA: Ryko; 1986.

Rogoff, Gordon. "America Screened". *Village Voice.* 17 December, 1985.

Rosen, Carol. "Emotional Territory: An Interview with Sam Shepard". *Modern Drama*, 36:1(1993).

Rosen, Carol. "Emotional Territory :An Interview with Sam Shepard". Modern Drama, 36:1 (1993).

Roudané, Matthew. Ed. *The Cambridge Companion to Sam Shepard (Cambridge Companions to Literature)*, London: campbridge UP, 2002

Scevill, James. "American Grotesque: Sam Shepard's *Buried Child*". *1979-80 Humanities Dramatic Work as a Cultural/ Historical l Document. Rhodes* Island Committee for Humanities.

Schift, Stephen. "Shepard on Broadway". *New Yorker*, 22 April, 1984.

Sheridan, Alan. *Michel Foucault: The Will to Truth.* London: Travistock Publications, 1982.

Shewey, Don. *Sam Shepard.* NY: Da Capo, 1997

Smith, Michael. "Introduction". Eds. Nick Ozel and Michael Smith. *Eight Plays from Off Off Broadway.* Indianapolis: Bobb's Merill co., 1966.

Savage Jr., William W. "*The Cowboy Myth*," The Cowboy: Six Shooters, Songs & Sex.Eds. Charles W. Harris & Buck Raimy. Oklahama: University Press, 1975.

Selden, Ramon. *The Theory of Criticism.* London: Longman, 1988.

Sharett, Christopher, ed. *Crisis Cinema: The Apocalypse Idea in Postmodern Narrative Film.* Washington D.C Maisonneuve Press, 1993.

Sheridan, Alan, Michel Foucault: *The Will to Truth.* New York: Travistock Publications, 1982.

Siegel, Mark. "Holy Ghosts: The Mythic Cowboys in the Plays of Sam Shepard". *Rocky Mountain Review* 36: 4 (1982) 238-39.

Stambolian, George. "A Trip Through Popular Culture: Mad Dog Blues." Bonnie Maranca Ed. (1981)

Strinati, Dominic. "Book Reviews-Looka Yonder! The Imaginary America of Populist Culture by Duncan Webster." *Sociological Review*. 1990 May(n2): p.397-401.

Tynan, Kenneth. *Oh! Calcutta!: An Entertainment with Music. 2nd printing* ed. New York: Grove Press; 1969; c1969. (GP-603).

Wade, Leslie, A. Sam Shepard. (1997).

Wadle, Irving. Review. (Theater Upstairs Production). "Geography of a Horse Dreamer." *London Times* Feb. 22, 1974.

Wetzsteon, Ross. "Looking a Gift Horse Dreamer in the Month." *American Dream*. Ed. Bonnie Maranca. New York: Performing Arts Journal Publications, 1981.

Wetzsteon, Ross. Introduction. *Fool for Love and Other Plays of Sam Shepard*. New York: Bantam Books, 1988.

Williams, Raymond. *The Long Revolution*. Harmondsworth: Penguin, 1965.

Wade, Leslie A. *Sam Shepard and the American Theatre*. Westwood: Greenwood Press, 1997.

Wetzsteon, Ross. "The Genius of Sam Shepard". *New York,* 24 November, 1980.

Wade, Leslie A. Sam Shepard and the American Theatre. Westport, Connecticut: Greenwood Press, 1997.

Wilcox, "What is the Day of the Locust and Shepard's Angel City: Refiguring L.A Noir", MD 36:1 (1993) 61-75.
Noir". Modern Drama, 30:1 (1993).

Wade, Leslie. *Sam Shepard and the American Theatre*. 1997.

Wade, Leslie A. *Sam Shepard and the American Theatre. Westwood*: Greenwood Press, 1997.

Watt, Douglas. "Talk and, uh, music." Whew! *The Daily News*. 1979 Nov 15.

_____. "What's hot now." *Greensboro News & Record*. 1997 Jan 9 (D1).

Wetzsteon, Ross. Introduction. *Fool for Love and Other plays* (1988).

Wicke, Peter, *Rock Music: Culture, Aesthetic and Sociology*. Tr. Rachel Fogg. Cambridge, NY: Cambridge UP, 1990, (Originally published in German as Rock *Music: Zur Asthetic und Sociologie eines Marrennediuns*, 1987).

Wetzsteon, Ross. "The Genius of Sam Shepard". *New York,* 24 Nov.

Wetzsteon, Ross. "Ioduction". *Fool for Love and Other Plays by Sam Shepard.* New York: Bantam Books, 1984.

Wilcox, Leonard. "Modernism vs. Postmodernism: Shepard's *Tooth of Crime* and the Discourse of Popular Culture". *Modern Drama*. Downsview ON Canada: 30:4 (1987).

Winer, Linda. "A Recycled Tale of Cycles/ Shepard's '70s look at pop culture gets are write." *News day*. 1996 Dec 24: B2.

Young, B. A Review. "Theatre Upstairs: *Geography of a Horse Dreamer*." Financial Times, Feb. 22, 1974.

Zent, Maureen. "Olympic Artists Let the Music, Dance, Art and Other Culture Begin Festival Has Opera—and Elvis, Too." *The Salt Lake Tribune*. 1996 Jul 14: E1.

Zinman, Toby Silverman, "Visual Histrionics: Shepard's Theatre of the First Wall'. Reprinted by permission from Theatre Journal, December 1988, @John Hopkins University Press, 1988.

Index